by William Everson

VERSE

These Are the Ravens (1935)
San Joaquin (1939)
The Masculine Dead (1942)
The Waldport Poems (1944)
War Elegies (1944)
The Residual Years (1944)
Poems MCMXLII (1945)
The Residual Years (1948)
A Privacy of Speech (1949)
Triptych for the Living (1951)
An Age Insurgent (1959)
The Crooked Lines of God (1959)
The Year's Declension (1961)
The Hazards of Holiness (1962)
The Poet Is Dead (1964)
The Blowing of the Seed (1966)
Single Source (1966)
The Rose of Solitude (1967)
In the Fictive Wish (1967)
A Canticle to the Waterbirds (1968)
The Springing of the Blade (1968)
The Residual Years (1968)
The City Does Not Die (1969)
The Last Crusade (1969)
Who Is She that Looketh Forth as the Morning (1972)
Tendril in the Mesh (1973)
Black Hills (1973)
Man-Fate (1974)
River-Root/A Syzygy (1976)
The Mate-Flight of Eagles (1977)
Rattlesnake August (1978)
The Veritable Years (1978)
The Masks of Drought (1980)
Eastward the Armies (1980)
The American Bard (1981)

PROSE

Robinson Jeffers: Fragments of an Older Fury (1968)
Archetype West: The Pacific Coast as a Literary Region (1976)
Earth Poetry: Selected Essays and Interviews (1980)
Birth of a Poet: The Santa Cruz Meditations (1982)

WILLIAM EVERSON

BIRTH OF A POET

THE SANTA CRUZ MEDITATIONS

Edited by LEE BARTLETT

BLACK SPARROW PRESS   SANTA BARBARA   1982

LIBRARY OF CONGRESS CATALOGING IN PUBLICATION DATA

Everson, William, 1912-
  Birth of a poet.

  Includes bibliographical references.
  1. Meditations.   I. Bartlett, Lee, 1950-
II. Title.
PS3509.V65B48   814'.52   81-21775
ISBN 0-87685-538-9   AACR2
ISBN 0-87685-539-7 (signed)
ISBN 0-87685-537-0 (pbk.)

FOREWORD

The word *meditation* has religious connotations and doubtless seems strange in an academic context. In the classroom the corresponding term is *lecture* and one who teaches is a *lecturer.* The monastery has its classrooms and those who teach are also called lecturers, but meditation is associated with the chapel. However, a meditation is not the same as a sermon or homily. According to a commentary in the *Oxford English Dictionary,* traditionally "the sermon was a discourse developing a definite theme; the homily pursued the analytical method and expounded a paragraph or verse of scripture." Neither, however, required the meditative method, which is closer to prayer but differs in its object. "In meditation we converse with ourselves; in prayer we converse with God." Meditation, then, is the art of talking to oneself. This is something everyone can do privately; it takes a special gift to do it in the presence of others.

It follows that the chief difference between the lecture and meditation is that in the former, objective knowledge is communicated from the learned to the ignorant. In the latter those who share identical views come together to reflect on the implications of what they mutually seek. In the lecture the teacher retains his grasp on all he knows in order to communicate directly. In meditation the art is to transcend what one knows by immersing oneself in the inexhaustible depths of the subject under contemplation.

The method is illustrated by an anecdote from the annals of monasticism. A venerable Master, invited yearly to give the community retreat, undertook to reflect on the Lord's Prayer (which of course they all knew by heart), dwelling on it phrase by phrase. The first year he meditated on the opening words, "Our Father, who art in Heaven," and the next year he dwelt on its sequel, "Hallowed be Thy Name." Thus the years went by. Slowly and effortlessly the essence of the prayer emerged as the Master, inspired by the attentive silence of his listeners, probed deeper and deeper for the implications of the knowledge they held in common. Finally after many years the prayer did come to an end, and when the old Master returned the following summer the community was abuzz with speculation as to what text he now would choose for his meditation. However, on the very first day he confounded them by announcing that he would complete his long-standing assignment by reflecting on the beautiful word "Amen."

It is a good story, and, I trust, a true one. Suffice it to say that when I left the monastery for academe the method I brought with me was meditative rather than discursive. For I had learned how concepts seemingly exhausted by endless repetition could suddenly, under the probe of intuition, blossom into life. I decided that if this method worked with divine truths there was no reason why it would not be equally effective with human ones. Taking a common subject, one of concern to all my students, the problem of vocation, I began to meditate on it as I would on the Word of God.

William Everson

September 21, 1981
Kresge College
University of California
Santa Cruz, California

,

INTRODUCTION

Birth of a Poet emerges from the poet-shaman's archetypal impulse towards orchestration of experience into meaning. Everson, Antoninus, Everson. Farmer, conscientious objector, printer. Lover, monk, husband. Poet, mystic, prophet. The persona changes, but the search continues, always turning back into the self.

The poetry of William Everson divides rather naturally into three phases, a division the poet himself recognizes and encourages in his volume of collected Catholic poetry, *The Veritable Years*. In the preface to that book, Everson remarks that his life "emerges as a kind of Californian odyssey" involving "three basic levels, making a trilogy of the work achieved." The trilogy (his collected poems) is called *The Crooked Lines of God*, and two volumes have already appeared, with the third in progress. The first book, which collects works written through the poet's mid-thirties, is *The Residual Years*, "residual" because "it suggests a man's early phase of life when he engages the residue of history, struggling to discover his personal identity." The second volume, *The Veritable Years*, draws together Everson's poems written while he was Brother Antoninus, between 1949 and 1966; the years are "veritable" because they represent "a man's attempt to break the residual power of the past, achieve union with a metaphysical Absolute possessing intrinsic veritability on its own terms, beyond the power of process." The final volume (of which two books—*Man-Fate* and *The Masks of Drought* have appeared) will be called *The Integral Years*, "representing a man's effort to integrate into a synthetic whole the dichotomies that have split him, the thesis and antithesis that divide the world."

In a sense, *Birth of a Poet* makes the same attempt. "The function of poetry," Robert Graves writes, "is religious invocation of the Muse," the White Goddess, and William Everson has been in the service of the White Goddess from the start. While he is a ranking Robinson Jeffers scholar and a triple Virgo (the sign of the critical intelligence), his vocation has not been, in the main, that of critic or teacher, but that of poet. Also, though he is steeped in

Jungian depth-psychology and has made a serious study of astrology, the esthetic which he has developed from such probings is not systematic; rather it has emerged from the inside out, to be added to, modified, refined, from poem to poem and book to book over a space of forty years. Yet like *The Integral Years*, this book is a work of Everson's old age, and like the later verse, the effort to integrate, to somehow get it all down and together in prose, is here.

At Midnight Mass on Christmas of 1948, Everson, who until that time had a rising reputation as a poet of the California Central Valley, had an intense religious experience which impelled him into monastic life. He eventually became a Dominican, and over the next years published book after book of poetry as Brother Antoninus, replacing his early concerns with man's relationship to the land with man's relationship to God. He became the leading exponent of erotic mysticism in the Church, and with Thomas Merton enjoyed a reputation as one of the two finest Catholic poets since Gerard Manley Hopkins.

After leaving the Order in 1969, Everson accepted an offer to become poet-in-residence at Kresge College at the University of California, Santa Cruz. Perhaps as a combination of his own lack of formal university training and the eighteen years he spent as a Dominican, in his course he sought to redefine the academic lecture in terms of that with which he was most comfortable—the meditative tradition—hoping to build a series of meditations around the theme of the poet's vocation. During the fall quarter of his year-long course, he would focus on the vocational archetype itself, with special attention given to the nature of myth and dream in terms of the poet's call; the winter quarter would stress the national consciousness, what it means to be a poet in America; finally, the spring quarter would emphasize the regional element, what it means to be a poet living on the Pacific coast, probing in some ways even deeper than his seminal study *Archetype West*. Each meditation would take on a particular aspect of the broader topic, eventually moving into the heart of the interior castle of the poet's vocation.

On the surface, this book seems something on the order of Pascal's *Pensées*, a secular journal of contemplation. Yet because of Everson's years as a Dominican, *Birth of a Poet* perhaps more rightfully belongs to the tradition of such religious meditative works as St. Bonaventure's *Meditations of the Life of Christ*,

Thomas à Kempis's *The Imitation of Christ*, and St. Teresa's *The Interior Castle*. Where those works focus on the mystery of Christ as a means of deepening the interior life, Everson's meditations center on the mystery of the poet and his call, his vocation. As a Jungian, Everson sees the identification of the poet with the Christ figure as crucial. A work he refers to again and again here is Joseph Campbell's *The Hero With a Thousand Faces*, the classic Jungian study of the hero in terms of the separation–initiation–return motif. Just as Christ works out his destiny through that three-part process (his separation from the Father through his birth into the world, his initiation into the Divine Mystery through a series of trials, and his return to the Trinity through his symbolic resurrection and ascension), so too does the poet traditionally recapitulate the Christ myth in the discovery of his own vocation. For Everson, the poet has finally, like Christ, a foot in each of two worlds: he lives a man's (or woman's) corporeal existence in the daylight terrain of linear time, while through his art and his dreams he constantly crosses over into the dark night of cyclical time, the world of correspondence, symbol, and archetype.

The following meditations were taped during 1975 and 1976 by the Audio-Visual Department of the University of California at Santa Cruz. Thanks go to its staff, as well as to the University of California for an intercampus research grant which aided in the completion of this book. I am indebted to John Martin, John Kidd, and Seamus Cooney for their suggestions during the editing, to Susan Schumacher for typing the final draft of the manuscript, and especially to Bill Everson for his collaboration, patience and care.

Lee Bartlett

CONTENTS

BIRTH OF A POET

I

THE PRESENCE OF THE POET

Meditation One: The Way In

These meditations are a probe into the nature of birth. Gestation, actually. Pre-birth. Conception. They are all without structure, provisional. A venture into subjectivity, into that realm of the psyche we call the intuition. For there is another world to be known, another world to be realized and to be lived. Simple and pure, it is waiting to be entered.

—◆◆◆—

We live in the world of cause-and-effect, the world of linear time. The other world is the realm of cyclical time, the world of myth, a world not of cause-and-effect but of concurrence. The eternal return. The whole of that mythical world is built on the principle of recurrence; there is very little causation involved in it. Certainly you can displace the mythical with the power of causation. We have done it. In today's technology we are experiencing the apotheosis of cause-and-effect. For there is something about cause-and-effect which seizes the mind, and we yield ourselves to it voluntarily, because it is so factual and so concrete. Yet, if you peer deeply enough, you will see that this also shares part in recurrence. What looked to be cause-and-effect is basically a kind of mutuality.

—◆◆◆—

We look to the mystic for his perception into cyclical time. We say he is *spaced out* because he perceives correspondences, and in the deeps of his intuition is delivered from the world of cause-and-effect. He no longer deigns to move his hand to effect something, but simply smiles. He leaves the world of action and enters the world of contemplation, and in that world is vulnerable as all defenseless beings are.

For there are different kinds of vulnerability, just as there are different kinds of passivity. There is the intensely alert passivity of total consciousness, the highest form of awareness which senses the weft of things and rests above the world of cause-and-effect. It knows through some sort of intense inner perception when the great cycle has come around again. But until this happens, we serve under the regimen of cause-and-effect in order to get things done. Action comes from that world; understanding sends us to a different place in ourselves.

—◆◆◆—

Birth of a Poet. Meditations on charismatic vocation. *Vocari*. To be called. We always speak of the most noble of the professions of mankind as *callings*. And there is a strange linkage between the words profession and calling. You are called, you respond, you surrender; and when surrender is complete, you profess. All of these meditations are an exploration of that equation—the meaning of call and surrender, the meaning of profession. These are each archetypal entities, and they stand apart from the world of cause-and-effect. They gain their power, their force and their truth, from a different principle.

—◆◆◆—

Your dreams throw out possibilities to you every night, the possibility of what you are to be, of the nature of your vocation. Every night you get clues as to your calling, the measure of yourself in your responding witness of profession.

—◆◆◆—

You are entering another dimension. The world of adolescence is behind you, and you are converging upon the innate powers of your simmering energies. All your inner consciousness is in tune with what it is about to be, and it is listening for the call. The inchoate abstractness of poten-

18

tiality lies there craving to be realized, yet no conclusive symbol has been shown to compel your assent.

—◆◆◆—

Every vocation is controlled by a symbol, and that symbol comes not from the individual but from the race. The human race cannot go forward unless vocations arise to constellate the collective energies into true realization. It is the race which creates the vocation. All an individual can do is answer the call. That answer will be effective only if there is a due correspondence between the call and the response, which is why it is so important to listen for what your true calling is. By this time in your life you have become so programmed into assuming what your capabilities are, that doubtless you've already made a decision about your future course in life. You've got an academic major and are under way. Don't be so sure. I thought I knew what was what when I was twenty-one, too.

—◆◆◆—

You are the agent of a supreme potentiality, and the inheritor of a unique set of gifts. Never before in the world were they created. There is a certain transection of energy which has reached an apex utterly in you. In all this vast complexity around us, each one of you is unduplicable, and each cries out for recognition. We who are human beings are called upon to serve that mighty potentiality in a conscious way, but also through the way of the unconscious. To respond is the thing, whether consciously or unconsciously. A grain of sand or the highest intellect—in its response each celebrates the divine in its own way.

—◆◆◆—

I am a Christian, but I try to speak in cosmic terms in these meditations. I believe in a Creation. I believe in a singularity of essence imbued in every creature from the hand of the Creator. Yet though these are my particular beliefs, the

19

substance of these meditations doesn't focus there. Rather, it centers upon a certain cosmic immanence which has to be recognized. If you think the cosmos is just a bunch of dead matter wheeling around and around in its own gyrations, a self-sufficient mechanism which just happened to happen, then nothing I say will make any sense at all. I am talking about the living presence of things, the unmistakable *quivering energy* alive in all things. Every form of apartness and togetherness is living and free, quivering and breathing. I bow before its majesty and before the living God, because the face of God is in everything.

—◆◆◆—

I believe that personality is, ontologically speaking, the highest entity in the vast Sea of Being which we apprehend about us. To that degree, the person is the supreme attestation of the Divine. If that makes these meditations religious, so be it. I certainly don't intend to apologize for my beliefs, yet sometimes you hear this course dismissed because it is said to be "religious." It's religious all right, but brace yourself. It is religious in a way you just might not be prepared for.

—◆◆◆—

I myself don't think of it as religious at all. For me, religion is worship. This course is not a venture in worship, but a venture in its sister-spirit, attraction. It is the other side of the coin. This is a strange thing, sort of like being in love. A beautiful woman will know how to be both active and passive; she will know how to stimulate and enforce as well as how to accept and receive. In this way I too am woman-like—I rely upon a certain magnetism to evoke a suggestibility.

—◆◆◆—

Vocation is like love—until it is awakened in you, you don't know what it is. When you are a child, you don't know what sexuality is, yet once it awakens within you there is no going back—from that point on you are a sexual being. The whole pre-sexual world is closed to you, and cannot be recovered again for yourself; you stand forever in your sexuality. That is the way it is with religion, once you are awakened it will be forever, and that is the way it is with death. In some way, the whole mastery of your vocation is a mastery of the mystery of death. It is an approach to that mystery, because in death all our purposes are subsumed into another dimension; we achieve in death what we opted for in life. From one point of view you might say that vocation, in teaching us how to expend ourselves, teaches us how to die.

—◆◆◆—

From the perspective of linear time we have a deep resistance to the whole idea of surrender. All its associations are repugnant. "I may be forced to submit," we say righteously, "but I will never surrender." Some time ago I was reading at Colgate. Actually it was "Black Saturday," the night Nixon fired Cox.[1] In introducing my poems I began to expatiate on the primacy of the call and the necessity of surrender, just as I do here. Suddenly out of the darkness of the audience cracked a woman's ringing voice: *"What's this surrender shit!"* Thrown back into linear time I was speechless.

—◆◆◆—

Nevertheless, to enter the cyclical world we have to relearn the ancient art of surrender. Our repugnance is essentially political, but surrender, as an art, is immemorially prepolitical in origin. Actually, our primary model for this is religious, but sexuality will serve. You surrender to God and you surrender to love, or there is no profound realization. It is the ancient paradox: you have to lose your life in order to gain it.

—◆◆◆—

21

In these meditations, the great cycles must concur. We move beyond the realm of cause-and-effect. We listen and receive. No one is coerced, nothing is asked of you. You don't have to make a response of any kind; the dimension is there, simply established, and it's as much your creation as mine. These meditations wouldn't happen if you weren't present to evoke them. Through them, we lose our separateness. Through them, we achieve one awareness.

—◆◆◆—

Even so, as we progress, I will say many things you will deny. With an involuntary reaction you will protest in your heart against them. But as I throw these things out, remember that they are simply ways *in*, not final statements. I will try to straight-arm you, try to jolt you. You must open yourself to me, even as you arm yourself against me. You must allow yourself to hear what you're listening to.

—◆◆◆—

Vocare. Vocare. The calling. A call from the deep of the night in the inner soul. The dark submergence of the soul. The inner being is opening its eye, trying to see. The inner nodes are birthing, flowering. Messages of supreme consequence, implicit urgency. The great cross-over point in your life. The Threshold.

Meditation Two: Identity

Cyclical time is very jealous of itself. When you enter its world of myth and dream, of ritual and wonder, there is an innate revulsion from the processes of linear time. Because linear time has been so triumphant in the 20th century, and because its masculine connotations are so pronounced, cyclical time will often withdraw in a deeply feminine way. Then when the painfully explicit causations are not permitted to connect, the dialectic must be sought at a deeper level.

— ◆◆◆ —

Actually, as suggested in the last meditation, the cyclical element of mutuality is inherent in cause-and-effect itself, and this is the germ of its own vulnerability, as well as the key to synthesis with the vaster domain of cyclical time. Only by the process of exclusion, by an enforced singleness of connection between subject and object, can it implement strategic causation, but its restrictions belie it. Causation, outside the narrow range of its direct connectives, has little power. The vaster dimension overwhelms it. As we deplete our resources to implement the last gasp of our technology, the whole cosmic vastness of things inches in on us. Actually, this Achilles' heel, this hernia in the groin of causation, lurks in the slightest of its tenuous connections. Reach out your hand to effect something and often as not you will err; something in the web of your sensibility goes awry. The innate division at the heart of things jiggles your aim. The intrusion of the cyclical instance is always shorting out the linear connections.

— ◆◆◆ —

In my own life I find this tension between the linear and cyclical modes interfering time and again. Probably some abiding principle of recurrence is accountable, but to my lacerated psyche it seems more hit and miss. Whenever I seek the thrust into awareness, into the cyclical reality, the technical means tend to cut out, something on another level nullifies the implications of what is attempted. For instance, when I go out to give a reading I have learned to think first of the equipment—will the microphone be ready? Will the sound be on? As soon as I get on campus I must seek out the people in charge of the sound system to make sure everything is prepared. Yet sure as shooting, the fellow's grandmother died that weekend and he had to go off to the funeral; and the friend with whom he entrusted the equipment got distracted by an interesting girl. When it comes time for the reading, no matter how thoroughly you've laid your plans, some deep divisive element begins to plague the whole process. Or perhaps the recorder isn't on. When I knew I was going to make my final appearance as a monk at U. C. Davis,[2] I sent ahead asking them to make sure a tape-recorder was set up. Normally I am indifferent whether or not a reading is taped, but this was emerging as one of the most important events of my life. Furthermore, I knew reporters would be there, that the event would be sensationalized, and I wanted a transcript of what I actually said. It was not to be. Somebody didn't get the message. But this is to be expected. The men of the linear world have affinity with linear things, and the men of the cyclic world have affinity with cyclical things. Verily, have ever the twain met?

—◆◆◆—

Many times, to the man of cyclical intuition, the very presence of the linear fact is disturbing. Cyclical time has no real use for history. It has, in fact, no *concept* of history. When everything occurs at the same moment as itself, there is no *process;* in absolute recurrence everything seems to stand still. But history was born with linear time—it is the imposition of the linear on the cyclical, the great drama of cultural evolution. Now in the triumph of linear time at its present apogee there begins the return to cyclical intuition. The rise of myth in our consciousness obtains all around us. The validation of the mythical aspect of things and of the dream world, now impinging from the cultural point of view, is an indication of the rise and recovery of cyclical time.

—◆◆—

This imperviousness of one world to the other takes many forms. Often, the most profound signature of cyclical time, the spoken voice, simply won't communicate into the linear pattern of print. We live in an age of emphatic transposition of the spoken word to the printed page, but almost always the real implications of the voice will not survive there. The weakest point of any transcribed interview is the injection of humor. The speaker makes an ironic aside which the entire audience responds to, but as far as the text goes there is just a little square bracket in the transcript reading [laughter]. There really isn't any other way to handle something like that. The page simply can't register what the voice is saying.

—◆◆—

In Joseph Campbell's *The Hero With a Thousand Faces*, he introduces the schema of the monomyth, a term he got from Joyce.[3] The monomyth is the cyclic pattern of the hero, built of three parts—a separation from the known world, an initiation and penetration into another world, and the return back to this world. Campbell scales the various myths, usually of a sacred nature, showing how each in its own way enacts the archetype. This is crucial to our understanding of the heroic mode.

—◆◆—

25

Generally, we think of identity in terms of some achievement of the self. When we can do something singular and become known among our peers, be set apart in their minds even for a short time, we gain a consciousness of our own identity, a sense of our uniqueness. This crystalization of self-awareness in our acts, our deeds of worth, becomes our concept of self. That is about the only way linear time can come to terms with the problem of identity. Singularity is a mark of individuation.

—◆◆◆—

In cyclical time the problem is manifestly easier. In the first place, there isn't such a crystallized sense of uniqueness and distinction in the world of wonder. People are more beholders than doers. Everything is ritualized, and it is not so much the group, in the sense of socialization, but rather the *participation mystique*. Whereas in linear time it was the separation between subject and object which was the point of significance, here it is the belonging, the connaturality between subject and object, which is the bond of being. In cyclical time the great wholeness of things is acknowledged through the participation of the one in the many. As the Great Wheel goes round and each individual becomes involved in its rhythm, one becomes subsumed in the archetypal world. This world is both rooted in society and in the transcendence of society. It becomes the subsuming power, where we live, grow, and have our being. The sense of self-realization comes unconsciously through the sense of belonging.

—◆◆◆—

If you can understand what participation as identity means in those terms, you can understand what a drastic problem from the point of view of linear time the identity crisis can be, built, as it is, on separation rather than on participation. In this whole matter of identity and vocation, one reason why we have to go to the dream life is that under linear

26

time things remain so categorically explicit. The drama of participation is forced to proceed on the level of action from the start. The child must learn to do singular things apart from every other kid on the block in order to achieve a sense of identity. We go off immediately into sports where everything is measured and gauged by how fast we can run or how high we can jump. Competition becomes the keynote to identity; and only in competition one can win.

—◆◆◆—

When your whole life is structured around winning and losing as key to identity it becomes, literally, a crucifixion. Nevertheless, this is what we are faced with in the world of linear time. We have to discover our identity under the auspice of an abstraction.

—◆◆◆—

One of the great rewards of being an artist, regardless of the medium, is that you can compete in the linear world and at the same time step outside the system. You participate in both realms, finding your identity in a mutuality of tone which touches both modes. But regardless of how brilliant you are on a competitive plane, unless you touch the other realm also, you will not be fulfilled, for it is possible to triumph in a competitive sense without achieving anything of abiding significance. Often an artist will become the idol of a particular group, and because of its prestige and control of the media you will be elevated to a position of distinction. Yet you may not really have arrived at all. For that is one of the greatest problems of the artist. Fame. Before fame arrives, the artist must first establish a psychic base through initiation. Here, the ideal of vocation becomes all important, for it is vocation alone which will give you a base in cyclical time and enable you to survive the onslaught of competition in the linear world. This is why the artist must efface himself in the cyclical world before he ascends to distinction in the linear one.

—◆◆◆—

We see this problem often in the lives of royalty, where scions are destined from birth to be the supreme individuals in their society. This whole sweeping archetype elevates them to a pre-eminent position before they have achieved identity in the world of experience. History dismisses such individuals as mere puppets or figureheads, utterly under the control of those who are able to manipulate them. Sometimes this is for the good of the state, sometimes for its downfall. In any case, there is no sense of identity in the person, even if he is the prince and will be the king. His vocation has not penetrated through to the other world.

—◆◆◆—

Separation, Initiation, and Return—the monomyth of human awareness. Everyone is going to have to go through it at one level or another, for until it is done identity will never be secure. I stress vocation as the way of entering into this process, but it can be done interiorly through meditation. However, Westerners come from an activist culture, and from my point of view vocation is one of the essential ways which, in this competitive world, the problem can be met, embraced, and resolved. For too often pure meditation leaves the active factor out of the picture. A person becomes a contemplative, and then isolates himself from the world to realize an interiority. He enters the cyclical world indeed, but when his return comes about, he has no vocational tools or proficiencies to help him effect what he left the world to discover.

—◆◆◆—

The presupposition behind these meditations is that if you can make that separation, initiation, and return in terms of vocation, you should be able to arrive at the end of the process not only with the inner journey achieved, but also with your tools and techniques in some degree of development. Only then will you be able to effect the thing you set out to do, even though it was a mystery when you began it.

—◆◆◆—

The problem of the break-in-plane is the same for the hero today as it was a thousand years ago, but he can't approach it with quite the same strategies. In the unconscious he can deal with it in the same way, but in the explicit world he just can't use the same tactics as, say, Aeneas used for the founding of Rome. You can go and found your own city, but our relation to linear time has changed and it just doesn't work the way it worked for Aeneas.

—◆◆◆—

This is the mystery, the risk, and the threat. Because that threshold-crossing is an archetype and is symbolically *active* in its own way, it throws up the monsters in the monomyth which are proportionate for you in this time and this place. But you can't see the threshold; you can only experience it. You must go through that matrix on *its* terms, not on your own. This is why it takes an heroic consciousness to do it. And it takes, too, a bit of desperation pushing from behind. When things close off behind you, you have only one way to go—ahead to the archetype.

—◆◆◆—

I became a poet because this vocation carried me through the break-in-plane, became the solution to my identity. But that is just the beginning. It is a long process, an entry into a desert zone which is a very broad expanse. Suppose you grew up in Los Angeles and started East and then suddenly hit the desert. You've got a long way to go. Sometimes that desert has a mighty tempting oasis, a Las Vegas, lurking there among its nooks and crannies. There are more beguiling places in the desert than you'd like to imagine, and many times you will fall into the never-never land of slumber. You must make sure that you get beyond Las Vegas.

29

—◆◆—

Las Vegas cannot be overcome unless you have something to do. You can renounce it, leave it behind you, go around the outskirts of it, but sooner or later there is going to be another version of it, right up at the next oasis ahead. When you get parched enough you are going to go into that place and get something to satisfy your thirst, take a rest from the ordeal of the long migration.

—◆◆—

I have stopped at many oases in my life. Vocation is the force that carries you beyond them, that won't let you rest, that seizes you and possesses you and carries you along. When you have your vocation, you have your archetype. Like calls to like, and dislike spits at dislike. No matter how much you try to rest in an oasis, sooner or later it evacuates you. You might be willing to settle for everything it offers because you're tired of the journey, but at that time something else comes to your rescue, the innate disposition of what you are. It is your vocation, and that is what sets you apart and says *go.* You feel that spiritual craving which is a different thing from either sensual or intellectual thirst; that spiritual thirst to be with your own kind, to associate with them and participate with them, sends you once again on your way across the desert.

—◆◆—

Sometimes you will never find your own kind. Some archetypes are like that. The hunger of your heart for its kind is never quenched. Nevertheless, you create for your own even if you've never found them in your physical life. Eventually *they* will find you. Many an artist, lonely and unrecognized or unappreciated in his time, thought to be mad, is eventually united with his own kind. Emily Dickinson is a perfect example. She was a beautiful spirit, yet the few people who knew of her poetry thought she was cracked, and she may well have been. But she was cracked in a beautiful way, a scintillating and angelic way. Crazy like an angel was Emily Dickinson. All around her the great complacent life of New England, going about its Victorian fulfillment on the New Continent, ordained the triumph of the industrial world. The great Victorian world of opulence and material wealth was basking in the ambience of America, while right down in the node of its guts, like a pearl in an oyster, one creative intelligence sang and talked to her own kind, which just happened to be a host of angels.

—◆◆◆—

Emily Dickinson wasn't mad, because she possessed her vocation. It enabled her to skate on the brink of insanity, yet retain her complete integrity. All the hell the Victorians were trying to deny through the accumulation of wealth she lived out in her beautifully skeptical intelligence. She took nothing for granted, but possessed the sovereign right to see everything to its essential core.

—◆◆◆—

I didn't go about it that way myself. Even after eighteen years in a monastery, I can't claim to be an angelic man. I don't have the particular kind of vision called the *angelic intelligence.* I am a sensual man, and my sensual needs become the law of my being. I live out the physical vibration as the impulse of my life, and through its exercise, rather than its denial, I fulfill what I am. That's a terrible thing. And a terrible beauty.

—◆◆◆—

In a way, to be an Emily Dickinson would have solved so much in my life, because she lived a dual role, a hermit in a household. She had the temperament for it. I thought that to be a monk and a celibate, and to exercise my vocation as a poet in a monastery, could solve the problem for me—that the sensual factor would be converted into the intellectual

31

and the imaginative one and sustained there. For many years it did sustain me. But the break-in-plane, the break-in-plane! Suddenly the great hand reached through that veil and seized me, pulled me back into the world.

—◆◆◆—

Separation, Initiation, and Return. But the break-in-plane that archetype, persists there as inscrutable as ever. As many times as I've been through it I know nothing of it. Christians call it the consequence of Original Sin; the loss of that subsuming beatitude which enabled man to see both sides, and to live in perfect harmony and disposition with no kind of break. But we opted for another world, and now we spend our days flipping out, from the linear to the cyclical and back again.

—◆◆◆—

All great art is gauged on that dimension, and, setting aside the collective liturgies, and the detachment of contemplation, it is the most direct means we have of bringing us back into harmony. Art is the aperture through which we slip inside the threshold, momentarily at least, to gain a vision of the two points of view as they come together.

—◆◆◆—

I am trembling a bit just going through all of this in my head. I'm like an escapee who trembles when he reapproaches the Iron Curtain, with all its barb wire, electrical charges, and hidden explosives. But the Iron Curtain is really only a symbol of that threshold. We must penetrate it in order to obtain our wholeness, our beatitude. You possess both worlds within you, they are each yours by right. You must not let that outside world, with its emphasis on the linear, deny you your deeper self, which is of the cyclical mode. Your course in life must always be to hold both realms in your being. Your vocation is the process by which you bring them together.

32

Meditation Three:
The Ethos of the Dream

In this meditation I mean to dwell on what I call the ethos of the dream. Ethos is one of those beautiful words you use when you have to evoke intangible factors, qualities that can't be precisely pinpointed. I'll be using it a lot. I remember I was reading at Ellensberg State in central Washington many years ago, in the late fifties, before the "new consciousness" had begun to take. In the question period after the reading a youth stood up in the audience and asked belligerently: "First you called it *ethos* and then you called it *mystique* and then you called it *charisma*, but what I want to know is, what are you going to call it *next!*" The audience gasped and chuckled embarrassedly. I paced the platform a bit letting the implications sink in. Then I turned and said, "Look, son. If that's the way you heard it I'm not going to dispute about it. But really, it's like a joke. If you haven't got the point by this time you never will." The audience broke up.

—◆◆◆—

The dictionary defines ethos as "the characteristic spirit, prevalent tone or sentiment, of a people or community; the 'genius' of an institution or system." The Greeks used it to denote the constitutive character or disposition of a man. I speak of it here as the underlying motivational intention of the psychic activity we call dreaming. Truly, dreaming has its ethos, its normative habit, its inclinational tendency, its "genius." This can be asserted of your dreams because it can be asserted of you. As you familiarize yourself with your dreamlife you will gradually become aware of the inner dimension of your own psychological tendency, your ethos.

—◆◆◆—

Jung thinks of the dream as a mediation point between the conscious and unconscious sides of our minds. One value of following dreams is that they are a corrective to the over-simplifications of consciousness. The dream is always there, correcting, balancing. Sometimes your heaviest dreams, like nightmares, are signs that the consciousness has gone entirely too far along a certain direction and needs to be brought back toward wholeness. You've committed too much of your energy, too much of your values on a psychic area which is vulnerable, and it is this extreme vulnerability wherein your opposing values are locked which produces the nightmare. If you are having night-mares it means your cravings and your fears are throat to throat. You should draw back and clarify the stakes for yourself in the impasse.

—◆◆◆—

When a disturbed person consults a psychiatrist, generally the psychiatrist will, at least if he is a Jungian, get out his notebook and record a dream. Then he will begin to ques-tion the person seeking help, the analysand, about the val-ues associated with the elements of that particular dream. This personalistic detail he will enter right below the dream, and then below that, at his own leisure, he will begin to delineate the archetypes he sees there. It is on the basis of these two levels, the personal and the archetypal, that the patient will eventually come to terms with his dreams and with himself.

—◆◆◆—

Every symbol is *potentially* an archetype, but often it might not register with archetypal force because of your temporal

34

situation. A key. What is it as an object? This key to my car, for example. What is a key in the archetypal realm? What is it in a dream? Almost always the key emerges as a symbol of solution, the possibility of an answer, perhaps the entry to a new life, a secret and mysterious existence which is being offered to me. But since it's specifically a car key it might symbolize motivation, or potential libido, the car as a sexual symbol. Undeniably a key can be a trivial thing, but not in a dream. Nothing in a dream is trivial, or it wouldn't be there. The more deeply you regard the contents of your dream, even the apparently trivial contents, the more deeply will they begin to take on their archetypal character.

—◆◆◆—

Beautiful light is falling across the world right now. It's been a long, cold, rainy season. A blessed season because it has filled up all the dry earth which the drought had left without nourishment. These rainy days seeping in have in one sense robbed us of our accustomed sun-drenched weather, but in another sense they have brought a beautiful moodiness. When you walk outside and feel the moisture in the air there is a dream-like quality to it. There is a warm-wet ambience in the weather right now which is almost erotic.

—◆◆◆—

Stephen Spender once said that adolescence was a kind of tremulous balance between the sensual and the ideal. Our dreams are always adolescent in that regard, as each one of them fulfills that prescription. Part of the relevance of adolescence is coming to terms with the spontaneous life. They say we older people have trouble understanding our adolescent children because we repress that period of our lives; it is the period in our past which is the most disquieting to us. For this reason when your own children reach

that age you too will find yourself having the least rapport
with them.

———◆◆◆———

Nevertheless, your dream-life always retains for you some-
thing of that adolescent character. The essential quality of
naiveté, which is at the core of adolescence, is brought for-
ward there. If you can accept that part of yourself, that
repressed naiveté, you will find that many of the things
your dreams are trying to do for you will be more readily
accomplished. You have reached the time in your life when
the ideal is sharply focused because it is so distant. As
youth you now don't have the urgencies of the practical
world that will have to be grappled with later on. Thus the
ideal takes on a radically disproportionate place compared
to later in your life. As such, that disproportion injects an
intoxicating element into your psyche, and you oscillate
rapidly between the ideal version of what you feel you
ought to be and what you really *are*.

———◆◆◆———

We tend to polarize the sensual as the opposite of the ideal.
This is a mistake. We allow ourselves to stumble into sen-
suality because we cannot obtain the ideal, then lacerate
ourselves because we have stumbled. Often, early in life,
this factor militates against permanent relationships, espe-
cially marriage. You hesitate to commit yourself, even if it
is to the person to whom you are profoundly attracted. You
go through a long period of resistance because you don't see
how the relationship can serve the true confluence between
the sensual and the ideal.

———◆◆◆———

Yet, actually, this is another way in which the sexes serve
each other. Each has a different version of the ideal and of
the nature of the sensual, but this distinction is also a cross.
With woman the sensual is somehow more mental than

36

with man, due to the symbolic correlation of her animus with mentation, the animus being the masculine element in the feminine psyche. This disparity of ideality between the sexes makes for that ludicrous drollness in our relationships, so necessary and yet so mismatched. Our fantasies, which are really dream-correlates, reveal to us this basic dichotomy. Is it not ironic that in the patriarchy, where the male is the normative carrier of consciousness, masculine fantasies are largely phallic? Whereas the female, who in the patriarchy is symbolic of passion, in her personal fantasy-life is preoccupied with the ideal? I have a macho friend who says sardonically, "Every broad I lay wants to be valued for her mind!" drawing his mouth down to indicate that as far as he is concerned it is the least relevant part of her. Whereas it is apparent that every man wants his woman most of all to esteem him for his phallic reach.

—◆◆◆—

O ludicrous disparity! How the sexes grope and stumble together, hit and miss, falling between the sensual and the ideal, hopelessly attracted and hopelessly mismatched! Man brings to woman his dynamic physicality and she searches his soul in quest of an angel. Woman brings to man her keenest gifts of sensitivity and intelligence, and all he can do is fumble through her clothes.

—◆◆◆—

The idea most difficult to accept, and most necessary, is that the dream is the agent of wholeness. Dreams come in the night and go with such little resonance upon our conscious life that it is difficult for us to see them as agents of wholeness. It is hard for us to recognize our lives, from a conscious point of view, in any such dream-like or mythical way. A good way to capture this is through the study of myth as the scenario for your own archetypal experience. The myth is to the collective mind what the dream is to the personal mind. They both come out of the same psychic dimension. But the two aspects of that psychic dimension are collective and personal.

—◆◆◆—

We don't really know how myths are formed, in the same way that we don't really know how dreams are formed. They seem to arise spontaneously, almost without any given point of inception. The myth seems always to have been there. You can trace historically the first written record, but that record is always formed long after its origin.

—◆◆◆—

I am never satisfied with my own dreams, with the quality of them or the substance of them. They never seem to tell me as much about myself as I want to know. I get especially irritated when the dream tells me the same thing over and over again, something I think I already know. I get angry, but the dream just smiles back the same dream the next night. It does this because I haven't accepted what it is saying.

—◆◆◆—

Dreams almost always deal with imperfections rather than perfections, and that is one reason we don't like to recall them. We want to be reassured, rather than rebuked. In our personal relationships, if someone is always disagreeable to us we break off that particular relationship. If on the other hand, a person reassures us, we find ourselves going to him for his company. But dreams don't do that for us. They show us our illusions and our inflation.

—◆◆◆—

Inflation is that aspect of the psychic process in which the attribution is falsified. The kernel of the positive element may be there, but we inflate it out of proportion. We move forward then on the basis of pride which will end in a fall. Dreams will often show you your own inflation, especially if it is sexual, and you must learn to read this. Almost all inflation is the sign of the lack of experience in a given field. In our endeavors to compensate for a lack of experience or a lack of knowledge, the psychic energy is always trying to fill us up through an imaginative factor. The hiatus in our experience is filled with a projection into that realm by the imagination. It is almost as if the psychic energy has to go someplace, and because we are so fastened on the ideal world we tend to over-simplify our situation. Our dreams are constantly throwing up the nature of this inflation, and then cutting back on it.

—◆◆◆—

Jung speaks of the shadow figure which emerges in the dream-life. This is the composite of all the negative factors about ourselves which we are trying to eliminate in our own movement towards ideality. Oftentimes, you can tell the deficiencies in your ideality by looking at the nature of the shadow figure when it occurs in your dream-life.

—◆◆◆—

Men and women tend to dream about different things. It is pretty difficult for a man to understand a woman's emotional life, even as made manifest in her dreams. For instance, the whole idea of the baby as it occurs in women's dreams is alien to men. It is for both a symbol of the new life, yes, but it is so much more potent a symbol for the woman than it is for the man. Does the image of the baby speak out of a biological need or a psychological need? It can be the harbinger of either one. It can either mean that there is a new phase in a woman's spiritual life coming, or that she is unconsciously fixing to forget her birth-control pills.

—◆◆◆—

All the great things we produce, such as our children, come from the deepest parts of ourselves. Often they go against the set of our minds because we want to accomplish so much by the act of exclusion, and are ready to make tremendous sacrifices. This is especially true of the artist. He is willing to sacrifice the whole ambience of his life in order to achieve a realized work of art. That is why you have to be very wary about burning your bridges behind you, even for your art. Sometimes you are so overconcentrated that you narrow your art by denying your life. One of the great things about a vocation is that it has the power to simplify your energies, but it has the same power to destroy essential parts of yourself. In monastic life you see that happening all the time, and it takes a very wise director to take a soul that is really striving and keep it oriented to its human nature. There is a whole great tradition in spiritual life in which one wants to throw oneself out and crucify his whole sensibility in order to achieve that realized point of spiritual perfection. The same thing is true of the artist. Once the artist launches out on his vocation and becomes consumed with the passion to make an externalized esthetic object that is completely realized, there is the danger of moving too far out of the human realm. The artist and the mystic share this tendency. The mystic wants to perfect himself, the artist wants to perfect his work. They both serve the gods of perfection, and they both know that terrible tyranny. To make a perfect object or a perfect life can be destructive. There is a brutal self-denial in perfection, and many an artist has died in the pursuit of his goal, as has many a monk.

—◆◆◆—

It is possible to convert those same energies into the family life. There are some families in which the parents are so committed to civic resolution that the children are crucified on the goals of the parents. In scholarly families you see it everyday—if the children don't get "straight A's" there is big trouble and everyone gets uptight. There is a kind of

40

cumulative familial narrowing of purpose, and in the end the child is forced to stand back and find her own way. She will bear the marks of that shaping all her life, but sooner or later she will have to decide on her own course for herself.

—◆◆◆—

The significant thing about symbols is that they all have that ambivalent nature which can mean many things. It is up to you to clarify your own sources of volition. What I want to do is to unlock my inner self and give you the key to something I really know, and yet it seems that I am just clapping my lips over words that have no weight.

—◆◆◆—

Motivation is perhaps the biggest problem in learning to write. The development of the dream-life is one of the best of all possible ways of getting you into the imaginative dimension from which true writing springs. In writing your dreams, you should make them as vivid as possible. Get the *quality* down. Remember that the whole essence of dream is the essence of mood. What is mood? It is the *affective* manifestation of which the dream is the *visual* representation. There is no real creative process without mood. It is a losing of objectivity to another dimension, a further loss of self, and it is from this loss that all authentic work springs. It is not possible to create without losing your ego-consciousness. The great thing about the dream is that it takes us into that dimension of mood. Sometimes your finest poems come out of dreams, or out of your recording of a dream.

—◆◆◆—

Once you are deep enough into the imaginative life, you can even train yourself to dream. It can be done through auto-hypnosis, as you find the key which unlocks the unconscious and then touch it. In this state of mind you can suggest to yourself that tonight you will dream about a certain problem. In the same way that you would go to the *I Ching*, you can ask your dream for a solution. I am not sure of all the tricky ways you read about to get into the dream-life. I have used auto-hypnosis to great advantage, but I am always a bit wary of coercing the unconscious. I tend to think more that the spontaneity of the dream and the fantasy is superior to the coerciveness of my need. Just because you need to know the answer to something doesn't mean that you are ready for the answer. From one point of view, if you are ready for the answer, it will be given to you; if it is not given to you, you haven't made yourself ready for it.

—◆◆◆—

The main thing to do is to familiarize yourself with the whole psychic phenomenon which we call dreaming. Read the dreams of other people—there are many classic accounts of dreams which are both absorbing and instructive to us.

—◆◆◆—

What about death in a dream? Does that mean someone is going to die? Well, like the baby, death can mean many things. It can relate to the biological factor, or it can relate to some other kind of terminus, like the terminus of a connection or an idea. Perhaps an idea has lived itself out in your psyche, and the dream will treat it in terms of a symbolic death. On the other hand, sometimes a dream does reach right forward and somebody will actually die. A lady lived next door to us when I was a kid, who once for two days was strangely aggrieved. The next week she got a letter from Europe saying one of her parents had died. She knew it was coming.

—◆◆◆—

Sometimes dreams are religious. And often they are increasingly religious. Jung thinks the most intense religious dreams come during the middle of life. He feels that in the evolution of the psyche we go out from childhood through early maturity achieving our career goals, then in the middle of life the spectrum seems to move on. Here the religious factor comes more and more into prominence, because by this time the life-energies have to try to find their way into the world of the after-life.

—◆◆◆—

The after-life is an ancient theological idea not much valued right now. There are many ways to avoid considering it, but will our dreams let us do that? They keep telling us we are headed somewhere. They keep holding out the possibility.

Meditation Four: Myth & Dream

Last time we meditated on the ethos of the dream. The direction we took made it apparent that there is a certain correspondence between your ethos and your vocation. In fact, it might be tentatively stated that only after your ethos has found form can your vocation crystallize, can your course in life truly emerge. That might be worth a meditation in itself, but today we are called upon to pursue the relation between myth and dream, and perhaps if we succeed in bringing that into focus, something of what constitutes your personal ethos might emerge.

—◆◆◆—

For the dream is personal, the myth is collective. Of course, many dreams emerge from the collective unconscious, but the dream normally addresses itself to the individual, whereas the myth addresses itself to the race. There is a locus where they merge. In fact, they come together every night, though the dreamer rarely recognizes it. But sometimes they impinge with electrifying clarity. These are the moments that bring a man straight upright in bed, wondering what in hell he has unearthed.

—◆◆◆—

History is filled with tragic episodes of men who have taken their dreams and have tried to apply them in an objective way to the exterior world, especially in politics. There have been great generals who have followed the course of their dreams to disaster. Others, like Constantine, have followed them to triumph. Always you will be tempted by your dreams to make a direct, material attribution to your daily

45

life. It is as if the dream has given you a clear insight into the shape of events ahead, but on the basis of that insight you will make choices which will often prove disastrous to you.

—◆◆◆—

When the aboriginal people dreamed, they almost always took their dreams to have reference to the exterior world and followed them implicitly. We don't do that in our time. We don't see the dream as a solution to the immediate problems of life in a deterministic way. Our whole approach to the dream life, even on the scientific level, is what it reveals about the human heart. If you do choose to attribute your dreams in an objective way, you have the witness of history to show how dangerous that is, how easy it is to mis-read what is there.

—◆◆◆—

The great lesson the dream teaches us is the lesson of ourselves, and generally it is not too favorable. The whole mode of the dream is to bring into your gaze what you are overlooking about yourself. That is why the shadow-figure almost always plays such a large part in your dreams, representing the quintessence of your dislikes. Usually this is not formulated in your mind, so you can't know it all that well. Often you will even mis-represent a shadow-figure, but other people can tell. I've often quarreled with others about my own dreams, especially in terms of a shadow-figure, but usually I've been wrong.

—◆◆◆—

The shadow-figure is the greatest teacher your dreams can offer. If you look at him or her well, and study what your needs are that have produced such a figure, you will begin to come to terms with your dreams. Somehow, the fear that the shadow-figure holds is in some way connected deeply with our desires. We project outward, away from certain

46

values, and we see with marked clarity the ideal figure that we would like to shape ourselves into. All the time we are fashioning that ideal figure, we are also fashioning the negative one behind it. It is this negative image which constantly comes forward and tells us, "I too belong to you." When you get an overwhelming dream from the negative factor you know that you are pursuing too hard an ideal, at too concrete a level, and that you have to back off in your search and accept some of the limitation that comes from that negative area you are struggling to escape.

—◆◆◆—

Learn especially the law of polarity. In the whole conceptual range, there is no consciousness without polarity. It is almost as if you can learn more about any subject, briefly and concisely, by looking at its opposite and seeing what it defines. It is almost as if we are standing here with light on both sides, and we look into the light, while the shadow is the basic shape of ourselves. Learn then not to be frightened by the intimidating figures in your dreams, but to ask what they are trying to tell you.

—◆◆◆—

One good way to look at this problem is in terms of myth. The myth comes from the collective unconscious, while your dreams come primarily from your personal unconscious, but they both follow out some basic scenarios, and you can see from this your way of entering the race and participating in it. You become the actor in your dreams, as if you were given the role of some Shakespearean character to act out. You would of course know that it was different in some way from your own life, yet you would be intensely involved in it. Its detachment enables you to participate with a most provocative intensity. In your fantasies, dreams, and what you write, you are able to live at a more intense pitch than in your daily existence. Through this intensity of pitch you are able more sharply to realize your inner needs and aspirations.

—◆◆◆—

This too has its own forms of jeopardy, the chief of which is inflation, wherein the ego appropriates a great deal of the power released through its first approach to the unconscious. Due to the way our psyche is formed, we make a break somewhere near puberty between the unconscious contents, with their childlike spontaneity towards nature, and the conscious mind, which is more deliberate and exact. We build up a wall between the unconscious and the conscious minds. The whole problem of penetrating the world of archetypal models is that you invariably touch a whole reservoir of psychic energy concentrated there which has built up too much power to be readily accommodated into your ego. When that repressed energy does come out it increases the inflation which the ego appropriates to itself because it doesn't have any way to realize its incentives in direct action. It thus fantasizes and takes to itself this role of supreme pride.

—◆◆◆—

You encounter the problem whenever you enter into a new phase of life. I saw it especially in the Order when novices would come in and suddenly set themselves with great determination on the spiritual path. They would accept a model, maybe a saint or some older member of the community, and they would begin to define their life after that particular model. As they begin to achieve a certain degree of sufficiency, almost always the devilish problem of inflation would rise. You could see that novice began to live a *role*. You can probably also notice this in your friends, whenever they have embarked upon a new course, such as becoming a doctor or lawyer. You say of him that he is not living in the real world, and this threatens your friendship because suddenly he becomes distant from you, off in his own head. You wonder how you can break the syndrome that possesses him. But don't despair of him. It is almost impossible to enter one of those new phases without a high degree of inflation. But when you see it in others, reflect on yourself.

—◆◆—

Often your dreams will release that whole wealth of psychic energy which has been building up over the years. Suddenly you too will begin to see yourself on a mythical quest.

—◆◆—

Myths are not simply centering devices, although often they do function that way. By centering devices I mean, for example, the centering of desire. In the sexual stimulus by which we go through the glaze of life, the panoply of sexuality, there is a constant excitement which is the fabric of life. Then suddenly in the dream it centers in and evokes a figure of ideal sexuality, the union of opposites, which becomes the focus point of all that diffuse energy. There is a moment of appeasement and release as contact is made in the imagination.

—◆◆—

The myth helps the dreamer in that it provides him with an objective pattern; it enables him to see something of the entelechy of its impulse. That is, if you do discover that your dream is the basic scenario of an ancient myth, suddenly the myth allows you to see the final orientation of that impulse which you do not then have to live out in order to know. In some way, what the race has lived through we are often exempted from repeating. At the purely physical level we must of course live out the law of biotic life, but at the imaginative level it is not necessary that the race keep redreaming the things it has already learned. There is an evolutionary rule in the psyche, and each generation is at the frontier of the psychic evolution of the race. Through us, the probe of the whole race towards the possible human future is being enacted.

———◆◆◆———

One thing myths do is to teach the basic paradigms of human life, but also those which do not have to be lived out again. At one level we will live out all those myths, although this no longer need be done for the race. Some myths we must individually live out to gain wisdom, but the race already knows as much as it's going to know about the Oedipus complex. We keep walking the treadmill of the Oedipus complex as individuals, but the race got off a long time ago. It is ancient history now. You were sent into the world to dream a *new* dream, a new version of humanity. That is what you have to be alert for and aware of.

———◆◆◆———

Often, you are caught up in movements within yourself. The myth can show you the teleology of that particular motif, and deliver you from having to live it out either in disaster or along the line of a triumph which was long ago effected. Suppose you had the opportunity to become the tyrant of another country. What good would this do for the race? None, because as far as the race is concerned, there is no need for any people to go out and live again that particular myth. The accomplished myth can here show you which way *not* to go.

———◆◆◆———

It is hard to learn the lessons of myth and dreams because desire is constantly falling back into the old slots, the old grooves. Nothing is accomplished. We all do it time and again; I still fall into those old traps and errors. This is especially true when you don't live an objective life. I put such a premium on subjectivity that many times I stumble into false slots, until something is exhausted in me and I stop doing it. But our compulsions are always with us, and sometimes we escape them only by living them out. Sometimes we never escape them.

—◆◆◆—

Another great thing about the myths is that in their intellectual structure they have a powerful shaping force on our minds that our dreams lack. There is something *static* about the myth. The dynamic rests with our dreams, the stasis rests with the myths. The stasis, however, controls the dynamic by showing itself as the model. It is a great stabilizing force in every dreamer to have a good grounding in myth. There is certainly no better way to gain balance in your own life than to study the great myths and to recognize them in your dreams. Even the tragic myths are stabilizing. The myth of Oedipus shows you how you hate your father and love your mother, and it can operate in both men and women. You will bring to that a varying degree of intensity depending upon your own formation, yet certainly the myth gives you a way of responding to those basic movements within yourself. Without some kind of stabilizing norm (such as the myth) for the unconscious, all you could do would be to repress. In many ways, the reason we have repressed the unconscious contents is that the myths have lost their immediacy in our lives, and have to be recovered in a literary way. But myths do have to be recovered if you are ever going to make that thrust into wider consciousness.

—◆◆◆—

You do need a guide on your journey. Sometimes he is an historical figure, as when Dante goes into the Inferno, and Virgil comes along to lead him into the hell of his own inner reality, where all his political ambitions, hates, and detestations are spread before his very gaze. Dante was certainly writing out of his hatred and his sense of loss, but nevertheless the honesty with which he wrote shows that his images were springing invincibly from his own self. All his enemies were in some way nothing more than creations of his own proclivities.

—◆◆◆—

To know the shadow-figures is one of the great ways to alert yourself to the enemies in your life. Right now every one of you has certain enemies which are lurking about—sometimes they are barrier figures, sometimes they are rival peers, sometimes they are rival lovers, sometimes they are people who are going to physically harm you or steal from you. This goes even down to the animal order. Certain animals are antithetical to you, while certain are friends. When you try to study the nature of your antipathies, sometimes you will be able to go back into the dream life and locate them in particular episodes in your life. Maybe a certain kind of dog scared you badly as a child, or another kind of dog was friendly. Almost certainly you will touch in that search the neurotic element which is constellating within you the energy which should be going forward into your positive life. They say that every neurosis is simply a hurt that has never been accepted. This is the trauma, the psychic wound.

—◆◆◆—

Traumas begin very early. The Austrian psychoanalyst Otto Rank formulated what he called the birth trauma, the basic trauma. Now an American psychologist has developed a therapy called the Primal Scream.[4] Of course there is a growing movement known as natural childbirth which insists that it is possible for women to have children without crisis, that no such thing as a trauma need occur for mother or child. In a way, however, it really doesn't make any difference where you put the trauma; even if you gently detach it from the parturition process, you are just postponing it. Escape all the pitfalls, as infant or child or adolescent, sooner or later a trauma awaits you. If everything else fails, there's always love. That'll make you cry.

—◆◆◆—

Traumas are in many ways our greatest teachers. If there is no pain and resistance, then there is no strength and no volition. If there isn't opposition to life, there is no energy put into life—you become just a leaf on the stream, going you know not whither. No one needs that.

—◆◆◆—

What all of us really want to know is how we can best meet the difficulties of our life and emerge beyond them. Gladly will we go around most of them, but sooner or later we know that we will have to face them out, center into one or another of the damn things. At the time we pray for the fortitude, the self-knowledge and the self-mastery, to be able to meet the unknown. If life is good to you, it will test you early, then when the big trials come down, and they will, you will know how to handle yourself.

—◆◆◆—

A knowledge of myth is crucial to a knowledge of vocation. In some way vocation is an enterprise, an enterprise of service or discovery, and the moment it becomes that, it becomes mythic. It is this dimension which changes vocation from career to witness.

—◆◆◆—

Myths and dreams, myths and dreams. From an objective point of view, all of it is the world of illusion. Both myth and dreams have negative imputations: a dream is a false hope and a myth is a fiction. It is almost impossible for us to use the language without falling into those connotations. Often enough we all call something untrue a myth, or we all see someone launched on a false course and tell him to knock it off because he is just dreaming. The paradox is that the world of myth often shows you the way through the hard world of reality, for this, too, is recurrent. Sitting Bull dreamed *many soldiers falling into camp* and Custer's fate was sealed. In its deepest essence that is really what a myth is all about. The eternal return. There wouldn't be any reason for going into the world of myth and dream if it didn't show us the paradigmatic models of the race. Myth throws back to you the nature of your hunger, not so much from your personal desire, as from the vast racial ambition invested in you.

—◆◆◆—

The beauty of the here and now comes from its immediacy. Dream and myth are beautiful because of their distance. The distancing factor in myth and dream allows you the dimension to make your accomodation to them. We are moving into more and more of an open field, psychologically speaking; the culture is progressively losing its basic forms. It is almost as if the great paradigmatic models are dissolving and blending away. Even in my short life span, I find the changes that have come in society to be staggering. Some of the things I thought could never exist with any stability in society are today taken as simple facts of life. Divorce is an example. When I was born divorce was fairly uncommon, and it was believed society could not sustain a marked incidence of divorce and still have any basic stability. Also we as a nation are dedicated to the idea of freedom of expression, but no one ever thought we could sustain the onslaught of pornography that is thrown every day into the consciousness. In my younger days no one would have thought that the wholesale violence which comes through the media could be sustained by the entire population without its going berserk; yet we live with it daily.

—◆◆◆—

These times are just the beginnings of the new age of open expression. Perhaps I have it wrong. Perhaps these are the last days of open expression and a new age of closed expression is dawning. If the totalitarian nations succeed, the first thing they will close off is the freedom of expressive individuality, for in those cultures the emphasis is on the group rather than on the individual.

———◆◆◆———

There has been a long tradition from the Greeks until today which centers on the freedom of man. The great stabilizing cultures, which are generally totalitarian, have always in their virtue possessed the staying power of the group, adhering to certain habitual patterns that have been proved out in the past. To liberate the individual to his full expressiveness without inhibition is always the most dangerous road to go. The ethos of the West, from the Greeks forward, has moved towards that goal; we are living close to its edge in the mid-Seventies.

———◆◆◆———

More than anything else, you must learn to penetrate through your traumas, to utilize them as the shaping factors which make you strong. This comes down to a problem of faith, and its function in the meaning of the exigence of experience. *You must have faith*—faith in yourself as a human being and faith in your creative destiny in its myth-like dimension. I think there is a strong relation between any degree of faith and the awareness of the governance of myth. To me it seems almost unthinkable to try to meet the pains of life without the requisite myth to govern that encounter. What the myth is doing is offering the ordering point in the factor of faith, for it is faith which takes you through the center of the trauma. This doesn't mean that you shouldn't bring a skeptical spirit to your own myths. Sooner or later many of your myths will be outlived.

———◆◆◆———

There is also the myth of your erotic life, as you become a different kind of lover in different periods of your life.

Sometimes those love-spans are extremely physical; sometimes they are extremely spiritual. At times you go from one to the other—from the physical to the spiritual, and back again. Generally speaking, that is what happens at the lesser climacteric, the age of forty-nine, when a man begins to do crazy things with women. The thirties and the forties are extremely beautiful erotic periods, whereas in the twenties you had centered on a predominantly athletic response to sex. In the fifties, there is a kind of mad passion to recover adolescence. You do insane things—leave the monastery and marry a young woman! You live the myth because the myth sustains you. It is the paradigm of your own evolution, and you become beautiful because you imbibe that beauty and accept it into yourself. In some way, to be beautiful on that level is holy because beauty is wholeness. At that point, the holy and the whole come together. That is the point where God is.

Meditation Five: Free Will

One of the most terrible things about the occult occurs when the archetypes begin to sweep forward, and the human will seems thrust aside. The archetypes take over and specify along symbolic lines. Almost always, whenever a religious, political, or philosophical movement begins to wrestle with the human condition, it relegates the occult to a background position because of the problem of free will. Great nations and great religions seek to determine their own ethos by hewing out a cultural and speculative future. The great problem always is, to what extent do we really have free will to confront the compulsions and motivations that are hitting at us? No one has ever really solved that problem, primarily because theologians begin with the premise that man does have free will and that man has control of his fate. It is only on such an hypothesis that a culture can go forward. Yet always, the occult is standing behind that assumption with its great presences which preside over human destiny. Though they are driven into the background, or even underground, they still seem to maintain a hold on the popular imagination through superstition. In other ages, such as our age now, they begin to surface once more and be accepted by the public at large. As an individual, what do you do about it in your own life?

—◆◆◆—

Last night I was looking at the horoscope of Maria Montessori, the great founder of the Montessori Movement in child education.[5] She emerged in the 1920s with revolutionary theories about child education, and was immediately put down because she would not deny that she had a child out of wedlock. The populace of that time were not about to commit their children to a woman they thought to have loose morals. Their cry was that *this* shows what such freedom leads to, and her works were denigrated and attacked. Over the years, however, her ideas have sustained a powerful educational movement. Anyway, as I looked at her horoscope and read the little write-up under it, I saw that the key ingredient in her chart was the Sabian symbol, *children playing on a rug.* Suppose she had not wanted to get involved in the vocation of child rearing? Well, seeing those children on the rug may not seem like much to you, but to me it was mind-blowing that a revolutionary career could be evolved around a symbolic direction that pertinent. Out of three hundred and sixty symbols, hers was *children playing on a rug.*

—◆◆—

Was this destiny? It comes home to you with crushing force because when you look at your own chart you see just such specifications as that. In mine the key degree reads *the profile of a man suggesting the shape of his country.* What kind of God-awful specification is that? How do I cope with that? What am I to do about it? Am I to drop all my other concerns and start bracing myself for a super-patriotic role? Something is at work there, but I don't know how to begin. I do know it is the same archetype as Hawthorne's "The Great Stone Face."[6] I haven't read that story since grammar school. Why not? What do I fear to find out about myself and my destiny?

—◆◆—

When you discover your vocation, when your energies find their focus and you are off and away, that is a force within you, but it is not specified in terms of subject matter. This is of course where the root problem of the vocation comes in, the problem of the subject matter. Once you are a poet, what then is it going to be—politics, nature, religion? You can be any kind of poet, but which type will you choose? If you think you can run back to your horoscope to find that out I wish you luck. In my own case, I want to have enough free will to chart that course myself. But will it be permitted me?

—◆◆◆—

The adage astrologers use to protect themselves is that the stars impel, they do not compel. I don't think astrology is based on a cause-and-effect relationship between the planets and human actions. There is a different principle at work there, more in the nature of a correspondence or synchronicity. There is something greater than either the stars or myself at work, some tendency toward order.

—◆◆◆—

Generally, the problem of free will is tackled by both philosophers and theologians. It is easier for a theologian than for a philosopher because the theologian usually works under the principle of revelation, where the philosopher has to work with the data of experience which is limited to the human condition. Aristotle believed that man had both free will and an immortal soul. The fact that human kind is capable of pure abstraction meant that some part of him is removed from the material continuum. Some part of the soul, he believed, is beyond the law of cause-and-effect, and this indicates the presence of a free and immortal spirit, a being not subject to disintegration and change.

—◆◆◆—

59

A theologian attributes man's free will to the will of God, and that is a lot easier to live with because it doesn't have to stand upon the verification of proofs, but rather stands upon the principle of faith. Even there, however, the problem is still insoluble. To what extent is human will free? To what extent is it overborne by the will of God? How can both human will be free and God's will be supreme? Even the greatest theologians have not been able to answer these questions. They all admit that in the end we are faced with a mystery.

—◆◆◆—

After spending years in the monastery on a spiritual quest, the answer to the problem of free will seemed to me to reside in the contemplative dimension. Some of the great mystics have placed it there—Nicholas of Cusa,[7] for instance—rather than trying to battle out the zig-zags of cause-and-effect. Man has the capacity to contemplate the things that happen to him, and therefore can find resolution through the contemplative aspect of mind, the deepest realm of the spirit. "What has to be taken, take with mind wide." My entry into religion did not dislodge that truth I had found early on, but confirmed it.

—◆◆◆—

Somehow we must shift the emphasis from the self, the ego, to the race itself. Your wisdom is limited, but the racial wisdom comes up with mythical solutions which are consonant with the mythical origins of the race. The most profound knowledge is self-knowledge, and almost all traumas are instruments of your own increase in self-awareness. To be raised for eighteen years utterly in the school of cause-and-effect and then suddenly through the crisis in your life, the trauma, to be impelled to relate to another principle of existence is a difficult thing. Somehow this is only done through recourse to a mode of being which transcends cause-and-effect.

—◆◆◆—

There is a current school of psychology, Behaviorism, which seeks to reduce everything to cause-and-effect, denying that any part of man is unconditioned. It has a strong following. Its exponents increase data through their experiments and drop deeper and deeper in the modes of conditioning. Yet in the end, their position is absurd. They do serve the race, however, in showing the many ways we are conditioned. Many of the acts we take to be spontaneous decisions are indeed conditioned reflexes. We are reactive at depths far below our perception of stimuli.

—◆◆◆—

From the point of view of the mystic or the contemplative, the Behaviorists are not all that threatening. The deeper you go into contemplation, the more you realize that the whole power that sustains you is coming from a place removed from your own ego. The trans-egoistic world is the world of the spirit. Goethe said that he had never heard of a crime that he wasn't capable of committing. I must have been in my late twenties when I first heard that; I was shocked by it because I could think of plenty of crimes I didn't feel capable of committing. Now at the age of sixty-three I agree with Goethe. This fills me with a kind of wonder because of what it says about my freedom of will. If I don't *intend* to commit a crime, yet I do commit it, what does that say about freedom of will? What does that say about judgment and damnation?

—◆◆◆—

On a cosmic level, the meaning in all violation is an increase in awareness. Any violence has its meaning—it is never done for nothing. The reason for violent acts is always capable of falling into that perspective which brings it into comprehension. Somehow, before the violations of life, you have to reach down into your being and find your relation to them. You can't permit them to throw you. You have to grope for the meaning. Not the *reason* but the *meaning*. There are many ways to do this. The religious way says that if God permits something to happen, then God understands it. You can go a long way on that kind of attitude. I remember after the first H-bomb when everyone was so stunned, digging those pitiful little shelters in their backyards, an old lay brother told me, "That H-bomb can't do any more damage than God wants it to." I almost died laughing at such a simplistic approach, but his reaction was better than mine at the time. I surely couldn't come up with anything that good. *The H-bomb can't do any more damage than God wants it to.* How about that?

—◆◆◆—

Probably the most sound of all modern day assumptions, whether sacred or secular, is that there is no such thing as a perfect man. The most wide-spread myth in all the world is the myth of the fall of man, the myth of a paradisial existence from which man of his own volition fell into the world of phenomenal fact. All the travail and anguish that man has struggled through from that point on stems from the fall. Why did God permit that? Why did He permit man to fall?

—◆◆◆—

Once, in the monastery a young scholastic fell asleep during a lecture. The theologian stopped talking and rapped his knuckle on the lectern. "Brother John," he said, "I have a question for you." The young man awakened with a snap. "Why does God permit evil?" the old priest asked. Brother John was confused and answered evasively. "I knew the answer to that, Father, but I forgot it." The theologian looked at him. "You forgot!" he whispered. "Here is a question that the greatest minds have wrestled with down the centuries. The theologians, the philosophers, the moralists, the mystics, all have pondered it and none has solved it. In

62

fact, only two beings have ever claimed to know the answer, God and you. And *you* have forgotten!"

—◆◆◆—

Still, even if you don't come up with an answer like poor Brother John, the way you respond to that question in your own mind is going to determine your solution to many things in this life. Your attitude towards it is going to determine a great many choices for you. Why does God permit evil? I was at a conference at the University of Colorado a few years back. I. F. Stone was sitting across the table from me. I was in my religious garb, which made him rather impatient. "With all the evil in this world," he said, "how can you go on believing in a God?" I was taken aback, but I pulled myself together and said, "If I thought denying God would remove evil from the world, I would do it tomorrow." He had nothing more to say to me on that question.

—◆◆◆—

In some beautiful way, it suits His purposes. My own hunch is that God prefers a *dramatic* dimension to the scale of existence. If there is no evil, there is no drama. Was there no drama, therefore, in sinless Paradise? Certainly the potential was there in the Tree of Good and Evil, and the stern injunction, "Thou shalt not!" Introduce, then, the agent, the serpent, and the drama begins. Choose any Creation myth you like, the core situation is the same. Suddenly a choice is made, and the serene world of cyclical time is shattered by the law of cause-and-effect.

—◆◆◆—

You cannot live totally circumspect lives—if you do, you will end up stuffed shirts. It is enough if you learn to respond rather than react. Response has a spiritual implication that springs from man's ability to say *yes*. In reaction, you might be meaning *no* but you still do it. That is one of the terrible things about sin. Though it may largely be a reactive thing, it is the degree of responsiveness in it which is the determining factor in terms of your own awareness. Subjectively, it is the precise degree of awareness that changes a mere crime to a sin. In the world of the Behaviorist, there are no sins, and that is fashionable enough. But I am old fashioned enough to assert my capacity to sin as the guarantor of my free will. The stimulus may not be my own, but the assent to stimulus is absolutely my own. That lugubrious cry from the Bible Belt is not so far off the mark: "The devil made me do it the first time, but the second time I done it on my own!"

---◆◆◆---

So I prefer to sin, rather than disguise my sins as virtues. I find a certain degree of spiritual freedom in it that I never sense when I scoffed at the idea of sin as obsolete. I'm not thinking here of Luther's "Sin bravely!" which has an element of defiance in it, but something more of the splendor of the drama with God. The definition of a sin is something which alienates you from God, but paradoxically, when you lose your sense of sin you lose your sense of He Who Is. To be forgiven by God is more free than not to know Him.

---◆◆◆---

Each age has its own sense of sin. It discounts the sins that precede it, which have already been lived out. We no longer expose unwanted children on the hillside like Oedipus; instead we practice sterilization. We no longer impress slaves; we prefer to exploit. Masturbation was for centuries a sin; it is now a virtue. It relieves tension, doesn't it? All civilizations do this—meanwhile they cling in their hearts to new sins, because sinlessness lacks punch. If masturbation is no sin what am I going to do for my kicks, rape somebody? Therefore I say to you, if you're going to sin, then sin, but don't call it virtue. That is the carrot the ass follows over the precipice.

---◆◆◆---

Which is not to say that you don't change in your attitude toward your sins, for you do, even as you retain your sense of them. You go through a particular phase in the spiritual life, corresponding to the novitiate phase, in which things have a really heavy taboo character about them. You'd no sooner break that taboo than anything. Yet after a while you find that you have moved beyond that proscription and eventually you find yourself doing the things that you would once have died to keep from doing. This same process, if you're not careful, can take you right out of the spiritual life and dump you down in the world, hardly knowing what happened to you. Then you start to rationalize. I know priests who left the Order and now boast of the virtues they once condemned as sins. But as I say, I myself don't do that, even if I fall into the same things. Their so-called liberation is too often merely an accomodation to a phase of the world.

—◆◆◆—

This puts me in the strange place of seeming to carry all the outgrown sins and taboos of mankind on my shoulders. Actually, the religious mind is very close to superstition on many levels. In fact you might call them the two faces, positive and negative, of the same attitude, religion and superstition. They both recognize the archetypal world but they respond to it in different ways; the sense of *attribution* is what distinguishes them. Precisely because I am religious I am often caught before a superstition in a way I am not prepared for. Then my freedom of action is impaired because superstition is reactive instead of responsive. But by and large I think the best attitude is a healthy respect for even the most outrageous superstition until we know something of the symbolic impulsion behind it.

—◆◆◆—

In conclusion, then, let me caution you that in your probe into the archetypal world you won't go looking for the truths of science. Science has its own honorable place, which is triumphant in our time, and I respect it, but that is not what we are seeking here. Rather what we seek is gained through the opposite, a relaxation of the distinction between subject and object. Your quest is spiritual, and what will be tested is your immortal soul, but tested only in the sense of verification, and to the ends of verification. Something must be reclaimed from the world of process, and this is what you are about. Therefore, you must expose yourself to the dangerous kingdom, knowing that the resources for your survival are intrinsic in yourself, the essential spirit. No one has ever been guaranteed survival of anything. All we can ask is that we don't lose our soul by giving it to something false, some mere process. Your freedom is your Light. In it you walk protected from all the powers of the Dark.

Meditation Six:
The Power of the Negative

We have seen a lot of the power of the negative in recent years in terms of the rise of ethnic groups. The Black movement seized upon the slogan, "Black is beautiful." This is an attempt to regroup energies back on primary definitions and change them from a negative to a positive factor in the public mind by directness of encounter. I want to try to localize this sense of the negative as a universal, and to meditate on how it applies to a charismatic vocation.

—◆◆◆—

The negative is a powerful force, but it is useful only in certain kinds of situations. In some situations, the negative can become injurious to your cause. Unless you understand the symbolic mode of it, you cannot accurately choose between these occasions. You will be swept up in the power of your own negative and become what Jung calls the shadow-dominated personality. Every time this type of person reaches a certain degree of achievement, he invariably tends to make a deflection and nullify everything he has accomplished. This movement is unconsciously motivated, but devastating.

—◆◆◆—

The centering factor in the vocation is built on a principle of exclusion, and it is this fact that has latent within it the negative capability. Every exclusiveness is built on a negative factor—"I *exclude* in order to *affirm*." It is this process of willed exclusion which is the source of the centering power of vocation for it enables you to channel your energies within an exclusive symbolic pattern. Because of the archetype involved, you are able to sweep far ahead of your native potential, as through you the racial unconscious is being evoked and thrown directly into the future. The collective does not have the power to save itself; only the individual can do that. Consciousness proceeds only through the individual, through the creative personality, then back down into the collective. The race can only go forward through charismatic individuals who rise out of the common level and go through a certain psychic process of crystallization. Jung calls this Individuation, a term also found in Nietzsche. As kind of a fruitful off-giving they then pour back into the collective the substance of their penetration.

—◆◆◆—

You channel your energies and you exclude. This sense of exclusiveness which pervades the psyche of the redeemer figure—whether he is a saint, a mystic, or an artist—is localized in the negative factor. "I am not as other people are. I am a man set apart." He has no real knowledge of why he is set apart, but he believes the truth of it. He is, therefore, both an object of admiration and fear to the people around him who also sense that he is not as they are. We know that same fear when we see such a person and draw back from his touch. Often we speak of a person with a psychic imbalance as one who has been touched. There is almost a religious connotation to it, as if one has been touched by God. We sense in that kind of insanity the power of the negative.

—◆◆◆—

We see this in great drama. In *King Lear* Edgar assumes the part of a fool, but in fact the whole idea of the fool or jester in the King's court was a recognition of the power of the negative. The fool was the only one who had the right to rebuke the king. In a well-balanced society you could afford to have your fools and idiots in order to keep the power of the negative somehow in play, validated in terms of the social ethos, so that the king himself did not lose his balance. If the fool wasn't there, the king couldn't rule justly; with the fool there to satirize his misconceptions and his own inflation, the power of the negative was institutionalized and made curative.

—♦♦♦—

Often you see an athlete utilize the power of the negative in the same way. Think of Jimmy Connors, the young man who is at this moment one of the greatest tennis players in the world. He has a bad image with the crowds because of his apparent lack of sportsmanship. He snarls at the spectators and quarrels with the umpires and linesmen. Yet he insists that this is not because he has a nasty temper, but is simply the way he keeps his psychic energy flowing. As long as he can respond precisely as he feels, he has the impression that he can keep going and overcome any obstacles by sheer spontaneity and force. That is certainly his archetype—he is not a calculating player, but he simply overwhelms his opposition. He maintains his force by the directness of his feeling. Out of this he simply reacts without inhibition. This produces a negative impression on the crowds, and Connors is able to capture that negative impulse out of the very tension of the crowd itself and convert it into energy. This is something quite different from being the shadow-dominated person Jung speaks of. Connors's utilization of the negative is based upon a valid vocation— it cannot be faked.

—♦♦♦—

Think of the power of the negative in terms of your own vocation as a defining factor. From that point on don't fear it. It is your vocation itself which gives you the authority to utilize the negative factor when it arises.

—♦♦♦—

69

Many times in facing an audience I've experienced that. In order to make a deep probe I've violated the expectation which the audience brought to my particular role, and suddenly I get a negative flashback. I remember one time in London I was reading in my religious habit. Of course the British can be outrageous when it comes to public performance—it seems to be their convention to heckle anyone who presumes to take the platform. I had had some sensational publicity in the press just before the reading, and in the middle of my meditation a guy leaned back and shouted out, "Christianity makes my penis shrink!" Well, the audience was petrified; it seemed to be such a breach of good taste that even their tolerance for heckling was overwhelmed. I walked around for a little while thinking about that, and then I turned and said, "I wish it worked for me!"

—◆◆◆—

Once the audience has conferred upon you the archetype of the speaker, he whom they have come to hear, whatever happens is in the palm of your hand. Anything that is thrown at you can be directed back at the person who seeks to disrupt you, and you can turn the entire audience against him. If you are not a speaker, you shouldn't try it; if you do have the vocation, you can survive anything that comes at you from the audience because it has conferred that role on you. I am what you have conferred upon me, no more. If I touch you, it is because I have been touched.

—◆◆◆—

The great thing about the power of the negative is that it inevitably breaks up the blandness that settles over the collective whole. It has a certain bracing power about it which cracks the blandness of expectation, and focuses the attention on something new, something unexpected.

—◆◆◆—

What but fear winged the birds, and hunger
Jeweled with such eyes the great goshawk's head?
Violence has been the sire of all the world's values.

Who would remember Helen's face
Lacking the terrible halo of spears?
Who formed Christ but Herod and Caesar,
The cruel and bloody victories of Caesar?
Violence, the bloody sire of all the world's values.

Never weep, let them play,
Old violence is not too old to beget new values.

That's a pretty heavy way to go. The first thing you ask is
whether or not it is true. You see how the poet works—he
makes a flat statement, "violence is the sire of all the
world's values," then he proceeds to reinforce his point.
"What whittles so fine the fleet limbs of the antelope but
the tooth of the wolf?" He calls upon the psychological
dimension. "What made Helen immortal but the halo of
spears around her?" Who made the whole Christian age, by
which we have gotten to this point, but Herod and Caesar?
There is a powerful, telling voice there, evoking violent
images. You can dispute the statement, but the images
come through with terrible force. They speak louder than
flat statement.

———◆◆◆———

In a way, it is not pertinent to quarrel with a poem on a
philosophical level. It is better to hold it as a given truth
and open yourself up to the thrust and the power of the
negative, which constellates within it all the dark material.

———◆◆◆———

Peace has meaning only in terms of violence. In some terri-
ble way, the more sharp the violence, the more certain the
peace. Why should that be? Why is it that in order to taste
the true taste of peace, we must have both experienced and

inflicted violence? Each of us must define peace through the inflictions of his own heart, through the aggression he has served upon others. The only way that you can really get at this is through a poem, and in some way that is what poetry is meant to do. The only reason poetry has such staying power in the world is that it can cope with such paradoxes, and body forth the ambiguities between the poles.

—◆◆◆—

The poem is a synthesis, making thesis and antithesis coherent. Opposites have not communication until they are synthesized into wholes, and the only real wholes are esthetic wholes. Until the esthetic dimension is given, everything remains partial, because the esthetic is the key to the final universality. It is a terrible vocation to live with that kind of responsibility. It means that your heart must be founded on wholeness, for it is the need for wholeness that impels the poet to make his great resolving statement.

—◆◆◆—

"Violence is the sire of all the world's values." It could be a truism. In some cultures it could even be a cliché. The Nazis made an entire political rhetoric out of it, and almost all the great warrior societies of the past carried it explicitly as a value, made a cult of it. They felt ashamed in the presence of peace, a stinking, rotten thing. Only the extreme of projective force, culminating in an act of positive violence, was the clarifying factor. I suppose the solution of Christ was to take the same method, but accept the violence upon himself. He invoked his followers to receive rather than inflict. That is the dynamic of the Christian message, although it was never a cultural norm in the way that the warrior societies made aggression a glorified cultural norm. But Christ dealt with the problem of violence instead of ignoring it.

—◆◆◆—

76

There are, of course, other ways to go. The Buddhist way is certainly a different path in terms of the demarcation of the cycles which eventually evolve into a dimension where violence is no more. But I guess if I remain a Christian it is because I see violence as crucial to the existential situation. There is nothing to do but either bear or inflict it, and I do both daily. For me, the Cross specifies the ontological fact of existence. It is written upon my consciousness with acid, and I am both impelled towards it with a kind of lust and revulsed from it with a kind of horror. I am only able to live a viable life in terms of that dynamic; the awfulness of that truth won't let me rest. The only way I can get at it is to write the poem which brings it into focus. That is my vocation.

——◆◆◆——

My relationship to the Church is extremely ambiguous at this point in my life. After years in a monastery, it gags me to go to a parochial service. *Yet I can't get it out of my soul.* No amount of comfort has been able to eradicate that scar from the core of my being. There is simply no way to cope with it in my life, save to direct it back into my vocation. I must make of my marriage a violent marriage, and every encounter a new rupture of the hymen. A new marriage and a new maidenhead, but this female in myself longs for deflowering on the altar and crawls back to be pierced by God.

——◆◆◆——

"Violence is the sire of all the world's values." The *sire.* Phallus. Inseminate. Stab. Crucify.

——◆◆◆——

During the war I was a pacifist. I sought to deal with violence by exposing myself to it rather than by inflicting it. That was right for me at the time. It surely defined my relation to my peer group, my generation, and I gained great strength from it. It forced me to contemplate, to wrestle within myself the moral issues that surrounded me, and to redefine myself over against them rather than in terms of them. I believe I met that situation with honor, but years later something in the Cross changed me from a dove to a hawk. There is something about violence which attracts, yet violence never accomplishes anything useful. The goods that men go to war for are never realized. But the reasons that we commit violence or submit to it are never the reasons we admit to ourselves. In some way we do seek wholeness, but wholeness is only apparent through the gash in things. The mystery of the gash, the rupture of forms, reveals the superior reality behind the forms.

—◆◆◆—

Men resort to violence to clarify something, but nothing in the world of phenomena can ever permanently be clarified because it is always changing.

—◆◆◆—

When I was in the monastery, exempted from military service because of the habit I wore, my poems were constantly dealing with violence. I was always impelled towards that incipience of violence in the sacral context. Always behind that was the lurking question, "What in God's name is He up to?" I found no solutions except in the resolution of esthetic form. No one can answer the problem of evil in the world, but at least the poet can take aspects of it in the concrete and find a point of resolution in which some kind of whole is born from the paradox.

—◆◆◆—

Somehow we understand the violence of our own time better than that of an earlier age. We go driving down the road and see a smash-up, and it is perfectly comprehensible to us. But if we try to think of somebody being burnt at the stake, it is incomprehensible. We understand perfectly how we could destroy 80,000 people in a single atomic blast over Hiroshima in 1945—a logical extension of everything we have created. But burning at the stake? Unthinkable.

———◆◆◆———

I have a great attraction to the American Indians, and recently I was reading about scalping. It came from the Orient, with the tribes across the Bering Strait, as a hair fetish. Deformation kept your enemy out of the happy-hunting-ground; if you scalped your enemy, he couldn't get where you wanted to go. Only secondarily was the scalp a trophy. Doesn't that seem like a pathetic thing? To think that by ripping someone's hair off we could keep him out of heaven? Yet, we say that only *our kind* will make it to heaven, because if all those others are there too it won't be heaven for us. How is that for the human heart?

———◆◆◆———

The light guitar trills on, trills on. The mind curls on the fluid melody, is appeased by its passion. Even there, listen to those dark undertones establishing the ground on which lighter notes flicker away. There is a sense of loss even in a perfect melody. It is inescapable.

———◆◆◆———

There is a peculiar statement of Christ's which seems to verify what Jeffers' poems was saying. In some way it even verifies the ethos of the scalp. Christ said, "Heaven is taken by violence, and the violent will bear it away." There is that undercurrent in all his teachings which suggests that complacency is the real enemy of the spirit. "I would have you hot or cold, but lukewarm I spew out of my mouth." Terrible words for me, a man who fears his own violence.

———◆◆◆———

Your dreams tell you these things, and there you live it all out. The scenario unfolds nightly before your eyes, the two tendencies working out, clash! clash! clash! You arise either from bliss or terror. In a late poem Jeffers says that if a man didn't have to sleep he could bear anything. In the same poem he says, "Who ever heard of a pleasant dream?" I guess if you had pondered violence as much as he had you would see it even in your sleep.

—◆◆◆—

The last book of the Bible, "Apocalypse," is probably the most unmitigated and sustained document of violence in all religious literature. It was written by St. John, who is called the gentle one. Why is it that the meekest men have the most extravagantly violent imaginations?

—◆◆◆—

Since Christ has somehow invaded this meditation and taken it over, I am going to end with a poem about natural violence as prefiguring the mode of crucifixion, the power of the negative informing the rupture of form as it occurs in nature. It is called, "In All These Acts."[9] Just as Jeffers in his poem reached for crystallizing images from nature to body forth his intuition, so in this instance I call upon nature to build up the groundwork of context in which violence can be specified.

IN ALL THESE ACTS

Cleave the wood and thou shalt find Me,
lift the rock and I am there!

Dawn cried out: the brutal voice of a bird
Flattened the sea-glaze. Treading that surf
Hunch-headed fishers toed small agates,
Their delicate legs, iridescent, stilting the ripples.
Suddenly the cloud closed; they heard big wind
Boom back on the cliff, crunch timber over along the ridge.
They shook up their wings, crying; terror flustered their
    pinions.

80

Then hemlock, tall, torn by the roots, went crazily down,
The staggering gyrations of splintered kindling.
Flung out of bracken, fleet mule deer bolted;
But the great elk, caught midway between two scissoring logs,
Arched belly-up and died, the snapped spine
Half torn out of his peeled back, his hind legs
Jerking that gasped convulsion, the kick of spasmed life,
Paunch plowed open, purple entrails
Disgorged from the basketwork ribs
Erupting out, splashed sideways, wrapping him,
Gouted in blood, flecked with the brittle sliver of bone.
Frenzied, the terrible head
Thrashed off its antlered fuzz in that rubble
And then fell still, the great tongue
That had bugled in rut, calling the cow-elk up from the glades,
Thrust agonized out, the maimed member
Bloodily stiff in the stone-smashed teeth . . .

                                        Far down below,
The mountain torrent, that once having started
Could never be stopped, scooped up that avalanchial wrack
And strung it along, a riddle of bubble and littered duff
Spun down its thread. At the gorged river mouth
The sea plunged violently in, gasping its potholes,
Sucked and panted, answering itself in its spume.
The river, spent at last, beating driftwood up and down
In a frenzy of capitulation, pumped out its life,
Destroying itself in the mother sea,
There where the mammoth sea-grown salmon
Lurk immemorial, roe in their hulls, about to begin.
They will beat that barbarous beauty out
On those high-stacked shallows, those headwater claims,
Back where they were born. Along that upward-racing trek
Time springs through all its loops and flanges,
The many-faced splendor and the music of the leaf,
The copulation of beasts and the watery laughter of drakes,
Too few the grave witnesses, the wakeful, vengeful beauty,

81

Devolving itself of its whole constraint,
Erupting as it goes.

                    In all these acts
Christ crouches and seethes, pitched forward
On the crucifying stroke, juvescent, that will spring Him
Out of the germ, out of the belly of the dying buck,
Out of the father-phallus and the torn-up root.
These are the modes of His forth-showing,
His serene agonization. In the clicking teeth of otters
Over and over He dies and is born,
Shaping the weasel's jaw in His leap
And the staggering rush of the bass.

II
THE AMERICAN MUSE

Meditation Seven:
The Tongue of the Poet

Among the diverse and intangible properties that go to make up that highly complex phenomenon we call a nation, perhaps the most significant of all is the factor of language. It is the cement which binds all the others together. Politics, economics, religion, law, medicine, sports, the military—in practice each of these has a distinct national accent, but all the impalpable ingredients that make up the ethnic synthesis are subsumed within the sovereignty of the tongue. It touches them all and permeates them all, receiving from them its particular inflection, but modifying them in turn by its unique predispositions.

—◆◆◆—

Linguistics is defined as the science of language: phonetics, phonology, morphology and syntax. Today's meditation on language does not concern itself with such things. I am not learned in them. In fact, I am ignorant of them, and, thinking about it now, I confess that I have kept myself aloof from those disciplines by a careful superstitious distrust. Is it not strange that one who professes himself to be a *word man* should be fearful of the science of words? But poets are like that. We protect our resources from too specific a consciousness in order to unconsciously register the native impact of which we are the recipients.

—◆◆◆—

But protecting your invincible linguistic ignorance doesn't mean that you should not reflect upon some of the properties which any concern with language inevitably entails. You might call this meditation "The Tongue of the Poet," but it is really the mystery of nationalism that we have here set out to probe. Certainly we will not wrap it up in any complete way. But we have to penetrate into it somehow, willy nilly, in order to clarify our relationship to it. For the national destiny is one of the chief preoccupations and concerns of the poet, and he cannot reluct from it. Despite his contemporary alienation, he is more intensely involved in it than are most other vocations. And the reason is his relationship to the language. The reason is his damn mouth.

—◆◆◆—

For in some way the poet presides over his people's speech, and therefore shapes the mode of its significant intelligence. Ezra Pound went so far as to declare the poet to be in charge of language in an almost ministerial way. When he launched his revolution of the word early in this century one of his chief platforms was the purification of speech. He declared that the falsehoods of politics and commerce had so corrupted the roots of expression that language no longer meant what it said, and he set about correcting this by developing precision as the supreme corrective.[10] It was useful and efficacious as far as it went, but from my point of view precisionism has definite limitations.

—◆◆◆—

Here in America we are the inheritors of the English language and it is both our glory and our curse. It is a curse in the sense that it is becoming too universal. We profit from this universality in many ways, certainly, for it places us within the focus of the future; but nevertheless it can only result in a certain bleeding away of lingual properties that should be hoarded and kept from debasement. Latin went through the same process. I imagine the Romans felt mighty proud when they surveyed their world and saw that all the ethnic groups within their purview were subsumed under the authority of their speech. But also they must have groaned over what was happening to their tongue. Goths, Visigoths, Franks, Teutons, and of course many more, all began to alter the Latin language according to their own unconscious adaptation of its once pure waters. And not only ethnic accomodations but religious ones too. Christianity profoundly affected it. About thirty years ago a group of Jesuit scholars made a new translation of the Psalter and got the Pope to approve it. Their aim was to restore the Latin of the psalms to its classic purity, and they did this by excluding any Latin word that came into use after the third century, A.D. But a howl of protest went up from religious communities around Christendom because, very specifically, what it meant was that all the words which had been charged with Christian implication were eliminated. You see how universality is both a glory and a curse? The Latin tongue united Europe, but Cicero turned over in his grave! Now English is going through the same transformation, and the British groan over what we, the Americans among others, have done to their tongue.

—◆◆◆—

Still, we have no other. We are not like Frenchmen, Germans, Norwegians, Spaniards, or Russians who learn English in school because it has become the universal commercial language of this age, and, equally important, the universal scientific one. We take it with our mother's milk, the menstruum through which our most deep natal responses are transmuted into consciousness. It is our tongue, and this is its glory for us, this is its power for us, its sublimity for us. We did not acquire it; it was there from the beginning. It is our own. It is what we are.

—◆◆◆—

Actually, despite the despair of the British, the tongue never was all that pure, and that's one reason I suspect old Ezra's precisionism. No other language is said to be so broadly based in its synthetic accommodations as English. Tongue after tongue has gone into it, weaving their strands of diversity into a compelling fabric. Within it we are all nations, all peoples. America, of course, is that anyway, for we are the Melting Pot, but even before our founding our tongue was the cauldron of the race. Doubtless that's why it has emerged as the universal language. Every people formed it; and all peoples can find affinity within it. This gives us a tremendous advantage, for we can leave the concern with lingual purity to the British, for they have the institutions and the history and the insularity to effect it. Whereas the opportunities are all ours. We have the tongue as our native language, our mother tongue, possessing it as unconsciously and spontaneously as any Englishman, but we are also freed from those preservational British resistances. Before all the peoples of the world we can glory in its inexhaustible possibilities.

—◆◆◆—

Nevertheless, the tongue imposes its own limitations, and we forget them at our peril. It is important for any user of words, especially the poet, to keep in mind the confines within which he works. It is terribly important to grasp the fact that in poetry there are no pure ideas, there are only words. Nothing but words, from beginning to end. It's all done with words, words, words. And you can't go beyond the words of your native tongue. What it can't express you can't express. That is the truth. No beauty it does not possess can be yours. You, rather, are utterly its own. It has you in thrall. You think you are using it, but reflect, my friends, it is using you. The tongue is your master, and this recognition must be the source of your craftsmanship.

—◆◆◆—

Spontaneous utterance deals with the potentiality of a tongue but craftsmanship deals with its limitations. You have to learn to balance yourself between them. Use the right hand of your power in all its tumultuous pouring forth, its torrential sound, its waterfalls of dissonance and assonance, its cascades of tonality and inflection. But never forget the left hand of craftsmanship always has the last word. It defines the line beyond which you have not gone, and are prevented from going.

—♦♦♦—

All poets of passion have placed their emphasis on spontaneity and palpable immediacy. D. H. Lawrence, for example. He stood against Ezra's doctrine of precisionism and denied it in his teeth. But in the end even the apostles of spontaneity must cope with the limitations of the tongue, and when they do, craftsmanship rears its unsubduable head. For all passion must come to a close, and only craftsmanship is the arbiter of finality.

—♦♦♦—

In this my own practice stands halfway between Lawrence and Pound. I am a Lawrentian in that my adhesion to the power of language connects to libido—not just in the sexual sense, though, of course, that too; but libido in the sense of the torrent of erotic and psychic energy that pours from the solar plexus. Lawrence, too, was a Virgoan, and Virgo is certainly the sign of the craftsman; yet Lawrence stood as an emphatic anticraftsman. The answer to this paradox is that Virgo also rules the solar plexus, and Lawrence became its apostle. In a sense he had it both ways. By passing beyond superficial Virgoan preoccupation with detail, with craftsmanship, he could touch the wellspring of plexus power and let the native penchant inherent in his sign take care of the tidying up process, even as it emerged. For despite his denials he was a remarkable craftsman. Any Virgoans in the room? Let me urge you to follow the way of

Lawrence and forget about the details, because preoccupation with detail is the habit of the sign, the glory and the curse of the sign, and you can't lose that; it's always going to be there. So follow Lawrence and let it all out. More than anything else the Virgoan has to learn to jump through his own shadow, and Lawrence is the special exemplar of that, more than any other of the great Virgoans—more than Goethe, more than Tolstoy—he grasped that truth. I don't say he was greater than they, for he was not. But more than any of them he confronted the inherent contradiction in the sign, and throwing his weight that way, made a breakthrough, as the halfback finds the hole in the line just off center and breaks through for a touchdown. If Samuel Johnson, the greatest Virgoan in the language, could have realized that truth, the course of literature in the 18th century would have gone far differently.

—◆◆◆—

But this meditation is supposed to be about language and nationality, the tongue of the poet, not about astrology. Still, sometimes astrology provides the perfect frame of reference in which to bring certain problems into focus, and it would be stupid to forego it out of academic squeamishness. In meditation insight is all, and that requires an unspoiled innocence, really, the capacity to employ examples and devices in a fresh and uninhibited way. Even if the whole subject of astrology turns you off, in listening to these meditations you can't afford to be alienated from the drift of insight by your prejudice. Consider it as myth. You don't have to believe in Olympus to profit by the insight of Greek and Roman myths, and you don't have to believe in astrology to profit by its perspectives into human nature. It is a frame of reference. Master its associations and you will find yourself thinking in unprecedented ways. I mean unprecedented for you. And even in scholarship, you can't understand either Dante or Yeats unless you know it.

—◆◆◆—

To get back to language, the tongue of the poet. What a powerful organ the whole idea of the tongue is—so phallic and inseminating! The poet is a man with his balls in his throat, really. That goes for women poets, too. A poetess is a woman with balls period. And words are her gysm. There's a word for you! Talk about the mother tongue! You won't find it in the OED but it is ineradicable from the language. A real four letter word. Semen has its uses, of course, its precisionist uses. But nothing catches the essence of creative spunk like the word gysm. It fairly drips of sexuality.

—◆◆◆—

Oh, the tongue, the tongue of the poet, source of his manhood, inseminator, begetter of multitudes! In the deeps of his being the magic fruitfulness of words coalesces and then emerges. He responds with electric sensitivity to all the nuances of the language. It is the quintessence of imprecision—potent, evocative, combustible, explosive. When the disparate ingredients of association are brought together a titanic psychic eruption occurs, and a poem is born.

—◆◆◆—

You are American. You speak in a particular way. No Englishman or Australian would mistake it for his own. Something of the sweep of the landscape goes into your speech, the continental stretch and dimension. The tension is established. Anomalies are set in juxtaposition and the spark blazes between them, igniting the whole. There is a multitude of discordant voices latent within you, aching for utterance. No people in the history of mankind ever endured such an inpouring of disparate influences, such an influx of conglomerate tongues and proclivities. And you were born with the mighty instrument to match it, the English language. Stretch it to the ultimate, make it wrench and twist with the strain of creation, but *use it! use it!* And when you have done so, taste the savor of true realization, true appeasement. For in language, use is action, and it is all. The only thing that can kill a language is rust.

Meditation Eight: A Sense of Poise

The mystery of being an American will never be probed completely. Every nation keeps changing and evolving through the course of time. It seems strange that there could evolve such a thing as the American temperament in a mere two hundred years out of such diverse sources. When we go back into history, we can see, even by the paucity of texts that have come down to us, that as far as Europe goes the Germans, the French, and the Italians were largely the same at the Fall of the Roman Empire as they are now. Some kind of implicitly abiding constitutional disposition is established at a given place. Partly by virtue of that given climate, perhaps by being in a certain place at the cross-roads of the world, or perhaps by being an impingement on the larger social life around them, people evolve in certain ways. This is one of the most beautiful things in life, and one of the most reassuring. When you go to a foreign country and sense what the character is, when you come to some glimpse of its internal coherence, its majesty of unconsciousness, you are close to the mystery of a nationality. It is like a certain animal species which moves with a dignity peculiar to itself—you realize that you are in the presence of an archetype.

—◆◆◆—

The mystery deepens when it comes to America because we don't have all that much history to sustain us. We are still in the process of creating ourselves as a people, so that everything we do is not just a reflex of something that had been done centuries before us. We are still in the process of establishing the pattern which other American centuries in the future will mirror and recognize as their own. This gives us an exhilaration and excitement, but also a strange recklessness and improbability about the circumstances we find ourselves in, a certain provisional character in everything we do. In some ways, it is perhaps our deepest keynote at this time.

—✦✦✦—

Somehow, man's capacity for physical action stands at the center of the American archetype. It really goes back to the whole idea of the hero, and the cruciality of the hero's role in the evolution of consciousness. The athletes whom the culture throws forward into the spotlight are essentially of a heroic mold. The public expects from them something of the symbolic role of the hero, hoping somehow to deliver us from our own inertia. Because the physical energies are so much at the surface among our people, the athlete, as the doer of the deed, takes a central place. Our interest in what he says really revolves around our interest in what he does, or in what he is capable of doing.

—✦✦✦—

Whenever you have a flat democracy, a non-hierarchical society, the ordeal of the hero comes under greater and greater stress. In some way, he takes the place of the whole hierarchy that isn't there. He has to move in terms of spontaneity and instantaneous response to meet the issue as it emerges on the basis of his potential, his own insight, his own capacity to respond; he has to overcome the crisis situation in the act of meeting it. As there is no hierarchy, there are very few patterns, very few received forms to go by. The institutional aspect of things is at a minimum. From the point of view of the poet, this demands the capacity to find words for the instantaneity of his perceptions—to set them down with all the truth and immediacy with which an athlete is called upon to meet the exigencies of his sport.

When you see what happens in the last three seconds of a football game, for instance, how men transcend themselves in an effort to reach apotheosis (to deliver themselves from the fate of the clock, the fate of time, which is cutting down upon them second by second), and suddenly to reach out and step across that barrier in an act of consummate fulfillment, it is a triumph of consciousness. The poet holds his powers in something of the same way. He stands ever ready within himself to make the same kind of realization in the esthetic domain. He will not be celebrated to the same extent, but on the other hand what he does is permanent.

—◆◆◆—

As an artist, there are two ways to go. You can shut yourself off from the world and live a secret life in the way that Emily Dickinson did in the 19th century, or you can embrace the world and live a public life in the way Walt Whitman did. Both of those ways stand open to you, for in a sense they are both stances that relate to the same archetype. Each of those poets had the capacity to pit everything upon the stroke of intuition, although they were drawing upon two different aspects of the body politic.

—◆◆◆—

These two points of view complement each other, and are necessary. But in a sense, they both stand poised (at least in the American archetype) upon the same verge—the primacy and the immediacy of intuition and the spontaneity of response. There are some cultures where an extrovert will take an introvert out into society in order to introduce him to the structure of that society and how to find a place in it. In American life that isn't so. The extrovert takes the introvert out in order to experience life in its spontaneity and its flow—to know it in its own essence, rather than to find a structure or a place in it. It is a thing to be experienced because its substance is validated in the act of participation. The introvert draws the extrovert back out of that world in order to verify the same factor at the interior level. This has to do more with the play of intuition and the perception of ideas and values, what we think of as experience in depth. Either way, we will be able to recognize and accept each other only because of the thing that binds us together—the primacy of the intuition and of the instantaneity of the moment of impression. Surely, unless that primacy is held to, for us life becomes chaotic.

—◆◆◆—

It is pretty hard not to get chauvinistic when you try to explain something of what the American archetype is, even to yourself. You think of the frontiersman, even though the frontier is no longer there. I think one aspect of the frontiersman which is not very often dwelt on is his poverty of spirit, his standing apart from possessions. He can move through a land of plenty, a great world full of potential, and yet he can remain detached from any part of it. He lacks that instinct to settle down. The part of the American archetype which is not the settler, but the frontiersman, is the part that has to stand always ready in poverty of spirit. It must be detached to meet any moment of crisis.

—◆◆◆—

As Americans, we seem to put our stakes on so many contradictory things. We believe that the life of opulence and plenty naturally follows our hard work. We think of this as a just reward for our productive capabilities and our executive powers. At the same time, we also have that frugality in us which wants to stand apart from all possessions. We are confused in our religious heritage. We think of our heritage as primarily Protestant, the work-ethic, God as a father-figure who out of His largesse rewards or punishes in a distant way. At the same time, the quality of our lived religious experience is much more immediate, and we walk around the earth as if we are the sons of heaven and have the blessing of God already bestowed upon us. We act as if we are natural-born saints, made so by the nobility of our landscape and wilderness areas. We have a naive faith that the sacredness of our environment somehow rubs off on us, that it goes a long way to keep us holy. We are always being confounded when our experiences belie this, and as idealists we find that our mistakes are devastating.

—◆◆◆—

A new continent was discovered in order to give an old world the possibility of a different way to go. We've had two hundred years to do it. Some may say we've failed abysmally, but even if we have, the ideal still stands there waiting to be realized. We may not be able to realize it politically, but all life is not made up of politics. There are ways of realizing things in truth that politics can't touch. One is the role of the artist. This doesn't mean that politics shouldn't impinge on your artistic vision, because it is certainly going to do that. But it had better not master it and sweep you forward so that you are no longer the poet, but the politician. If that is your archetype, there is no quarrel there, but don't let your bitterness about the way things are stop your mouth from speaking.

—◆◆◆—

An American. There isn't any other way to be, damn it, if that's what you are. It is where your energies are. You have to find the core of what it means to be an American and then get with it. One of the great movements in this country was the expatriate movement of the Twenties, when artists left the country and went to Europe. Almost all of them came back again, sooner or later. I know that movement because I once tried to renounce my own citizenship, but my destiny prevented it from happening. I spent the greater part of my life trying to probe down through the negative factors to find the living root which makes me what I am. I feel that unless you do find it, or unless it is found, your relationship with your neighbors is going to be void. It really doesn't matter how well you relate to the people around you, unless you can relate at the primary level.

—✦✦✦—

I would say that of all the aspects of man's experience, politics is the most imperfect. It is the least trustworthy and the most chancey. You can create a perfect poem, but I'll be damned if you can create a perfect state. Or a perfect city, a perfect commune, a perfect administration of any kind. There is a deficiency of form. If you could prescribe the form, and then force the ingredients to adhere to it, you could achieve perfection—but you just can't do it in the way you can write a poem or a beautiful song. You can achieve moments of political illumination, moments when you are caught up in a ground-swell and the people rises to its feet as one and declares its heart in a resounding manifestation of collective purpose. You can experience it momentarily, and in that sense it is just like love. You can experience the great moment of love in its transcendent and sublime apotheosis, but you fall out of love too. Then you struggle slowly to find that moment again, because you live with the memory of what was supreme in your life. All revolutionaries do that. They have gone through and have experienced the upwelling and overthrow of a tyranny, then have lived in the memory of it and have seen that vision fade. The corruptness of man is not eradicated by revolutions. The drivers change places, but the whip goes on.

—✦✦✦—

I think as long as man exists, Americans will be facing their future in pretty much the same way they face it today: a certain quickness on the feet, a certain genius for improvisation, a certain distrust of set formulas as the guarantors, a certain disdain for correctness as a guiding principle, a certain appetite for the new. Many tragic mistakes are going to be made by Americans in the future—the world is going to curse us more than once, and jeer at us more than once. But

98

nevertheless, that is the way we are, and that is the way we will continue to be.

—✦✦✦—

As Americans, the best part of your poems will not be their mastery of form, but a certain release of energy that is unpredictable, that takes the poet as much by surprise as the reader. You will rely more on energy than on abstract thought, the same energy of reality itself which gives the American his supreme self-confidence.

—✦✦✦—

There is a certain period of retrenchment that we are beginning to go through. No one knows to what degree we can exercise our talents and our capacities in the world at large the way we have for the last twenty-five years. We don't worry too much about that. There is a certain instinctive pulling back as if we've over-extended ourselves upon foreign shores. It isn't quite the isolationism of the Twenties and the Thirties. It is pretty hard to recall the appalling revulsion following World War I, and the cynicism in this country because of our participation in that blood bath. I don't really look to see a revival of that kind of isolationism in this country. At the same time, there is a pulling back and a re-assessment of what we are capable of doing and what we shouldn't be doing. However, this doesn't mean we have lost our poise.

—✦✦✦—

I guess that is the word I have been trying to get to bring this meditation together—*poise*. What constitutes the American's sense of his own poise as distinct from a European's or an Asiatic's? Where is the source of inherent self-possession? To me, my deepening reflection on the fact of being an American is going to be in some way a meditation upon that question. It will be an attempt to find the answer for myself—not to expect it in those around me, but to expect it in myself. To adhere to my American roots as my sense of stability in a world of change.

Meditation Nine: The New Adam

It is the experience of wilderness that is the archetypal American experience. It was the thing that confronted the explorers when they first hit this country, and the thing with which every generation has somehow to cope—in the material way in the 19th century, and in the psychological way in the 20th century. America's poets always seem to prove that. Somehow it seems to fall within the domain of the poet to solve the dilemma of the race in terms of its tone, by finding the modes to coil back and regroup around those primordial forms.

—◆◆—

When the Pilgrims came they had the collective sense of a chosen people leaving a land of oppression. They came to this country and found themselves in the wilderness, just as the Children of Israel left Egypt and were forty years in the wilderness before they could find the Promised Land. The early Pilgrims embraced this analogy, and became an intensely collective people in that regard. In fact, it was such a theologically centered society that it developed a kind of obsessive passion for a beatitude on this earth, but the rights of the individual were repressed. It took a Roger Williams to reassert the value of the individual conscience as it had emerged in continental Protestantism to realize its American version against the proposed theocracy. With Roger Williams, the first linear voice was heard in the great cyclical stasis of the Puritan community.

—◆◆—

The whole notion of a chosen people and a chosen land became an important force in America in the 18th Century, centered in the concept of the American as the "New Adam." This idea of the New Adam as a primary American archetype is still at work among us. It is a source of our power, as well as a source of our limitation.

—◆◆◆—

Even in our dreams, when we encounter the archetype of the New Adam, we have to realize its theological source and its theological context. This means a factor of *divinization*, implicit divinization, that inheres around the creator, the poet as the New Adam. Even with the disappearance of a personal God from our culture, the basic idea of the divinization of the creator, of emergent creativity consolidated in the individual consciousness, has its theological sources. It means that so many times when the poet approaches his subject, he is going to approach it in terms of that reference back to the New Adam symbolism, calling up the sources of divinity he receives from his environment. We see this theological resonance today in our environmental movement, for example. You have to be aware of it to understand where its passion is coming from, where its sources of power are rooted in the general population. How it is that a small organization like the Sierra Club can stand up and face the whole industrial-military complex, and time and again stop it in its tracks. I don't say it will win out, though I hope it will. But it has that power appealing back to a theological base inherent in the American syndrome, much of which is inherent in the concept of the New Adam.

—◆◆◆—

The idea of a New Adam was theologically expressed long before Emerson, but as a cultural force it really goes back to him.[11] He put a new twist on it and carried it forward into a psychological and mental dimension which went straight through to Whitman. Whitman was the first poet to emerge

102

as its mouthpiece. He was the first poet to take on the persona of the New Adam, the first to live it out in his poetry and to attempt to live it out in his life.

—◆◆◆—

This point of view literally drips with nature. It is almost a saturation with nature, at least in the human variant in nature, the populace. Whitman expressed both sides of that—both the populace and the natural wonder—but he wasn't alone. Thoreau was there with him. Thoreau says,

> He would be a poet who could impress the winds and streams into his service to speak for him; who nailed words to their primitive senses, as farmers drive down stakes in the spring [which the frost has heaved]; who derived his words as often as he used them, transplanted them to his page with earth adhering to their roots.[12]

That is pretty strong stuff. It has a shocking power even today. It is a break back from intellect to sensation. The vigor of it is what is compelling. "Words drive down stakes to their primitive senses." Marvelous!

—◆◆◆—

It is so strange, so beautiful, that those three accents, Emerson, Thoreau, and Whitman are a kind of concatenation of original inspiration. They somehow crystallize the American archetype in a way which exceeds one's wildest expectations. You couldn't have predicted it. That doesn't mean that it wasn't contested—Poe contested it. He stood up on the other side of the spectrum as the opposite voice in America. Poe is the aristocrat. He came from the Virginian culture, with its aristocratic predispositions almost insured by slavery. This cuts man off from the earth and focuses his energies on the cultural level, the mental and the psychological plane. There is a break between the roots of the earth and the ruling class when an institution like slavery is imposed. For the South this was fatal for it delivered it into decadence, and in the shrillness of its decadence it went straight toward the division of the Civil War. If the South had been closer to the earth, it probably wouldn't have made that hysterical decision.

—◆◆◆—

Poe believed the exact opposite from Emerson and Whitman. He believed that the creative work of art had nothing to do with nature, that it had no source in nature. Its source was in the mind alone. The greatest follower of Poe in that esthetic in this century was Wallace Stevens, who also believed in the supreme artifice of the creative imagination. The whole of New Criticism, and in fact Modernism itself in this century, is largely concerned with the radical difference between art and nature, rather than their identity. Certainly that springs from an aristocratic point of view. In some ways it is a tension between the native American archetype, which almost always appeals back to nature, and the European one.

—◆◆◆—

As poets, it is going to be one of the most difficult things you have to solve for yourselves. Just what are you going to do with that problem? The prestige of the arcane solution and its hermetic view of the artist as one sealed off from nature and humanity, as one who contrives superior forms and lives in the fictive imagination where the esthetic truth resides, and who becomes the supreme artificer, who, making the perfect work of art detached from the rest of reality, existing in terms of its pure principles alone, is going to tempt you. After all, Poe had a tremendous impact on the esthetics of Europe—Baudelaire took him up and canonized him. But despite that, as far as Europe goes it has been the voice of Whitman more than any other person which has shown what the aboriginal American bard is, the New Adam.

—◆◆◆—

be from seaboard to seaboard. New York and Los Angeles between them rule the media.

—◆◆◆—

The American West is masculine, while the East is feminine. The East, however, is establishment oriented, which is a masculine trait, while the West is movement oriented, which is a feminine trait. There is a paradox there. From the point of view of the West, the East is effete because it has become mannered, and manners are more important to it than fullness of life. If you think of the East in a geographical sense as involving New York and Philadelphia, you can sense the power generated from that quarter. Boston is to the North, Atlanta to the South, and San Francisco to the West.

—◆◆◆—

People who study culture say that there are only two authentic cities in America, San Francisco and New Orleans. These are cities where the ambience of life is based on natural rhythms, yet each has its own measure of sophistication and international feeling about it.

—◆◆◆—

It is difficult to get the East in perspective from the West Coast. One of the reasons is the antagonism the West feels towards the East, part of which stems from the fact that the West feels that it is not taken seriously by the East. Generally, establishment cultures tend to be cloistered and self-contained. They evolve their mores around their basic institutions, and they appropriate power to themselves, conserve it, and are jealous of it. Because the West is terminal movement, this forces the East to be critical, to develop a point of view from which that movement can be estimated and appraised. This means that it is always speaking in terms of detachment because the critical instinct is separative; it separates and divides in order to analyze and understand. In its superficial aspects, this critical spirit takes on a superior tone.

—◆◆◆—

In the East, there is the cultivation of relationships as the ambience of collective human life. The West centers on raw energy. In the East, there is a concern for appropriateness, while in the West it is not so much what is appropriate as what is emphatic. In its need to keep its energy going the West invariably fosters indistinctions. This means that new life is constantly being shaped in the West, but must go East for judgement. You haven't made it until you've proved it to New York.

—◆◆◆—

The Northern and Southern polarities are the poles between which this East-West opposition is enacted. They watch over the action. Whereas in New York and Los Angeles the pace is frenetic, in the North and in the South the pace is much more deliberate. The North goes about its steel mills and auto producing with great certitude, while the South enacts its ambience of life and conviviality of manners. The masculine and the feminine, the father up North and the mother down South.

—◆◆◆—

Generally speaking, the patriarchy presides over institutions and the matriarchy presides over conventions. The stabilizing element in the matriarchy is always the convention because that is what the children can understand, and it evolves through recurrence. The patriarchy thinks in terms of objective structure, while the matriarchy thinks in terms of recurrent patterns.

—◆◆◆—

The basic sexual symbolisms which I am discussing here are coming under strong attack today, and perhaps are changing. Only time will tell. There is the feminist movement on the one hand, which fiercely assails them, as well as a large urbanized element in the masculine world which is weary of them. I am trying to speak of residual mythic characteristics from the past which have been carried forward and are still with us in their vertical symbolic function.

—◆◆◆—

As a Californian, the East still bears a strange, paradoxical symbolism for me. I still feel its prestige, involved as I am in West Coast attitudes and the achievement of a West Coast culture. As a poet, I look for recognition from the East, and when it doesn't happen I suffer in a different way than when it doesn't happen in the West. All the East's establishments and conventions seem to be marked by an exclusiveness, as well as an elegance and a refinement of taste, that makes them seem impossible to penetrate.

—◆◆◆—

Between these poles, East and West, lies the Midwest, which is just as fixated and rigid in its attitudes as the North or the South, save that it is less defined. Because it is a midpoint, it looks neither to the East nor to the West, and it has its own kind of stationary character. I suppose, in terms of the sexual symbolism, it is masculine. It doesn't seem to have the feminine sensibility, even though most of its productivity is agricultural.

—◆◆◆—

These sexual symbols are difficult to make coherent in a democracy, which is fraternal in spirit and ethos, but nevertheless the centers are touching, vibrating, and melting. Vague and ill-defined as they are, such symbols are the cohering points. When you consider a thing like the Civil War, you see how deeply ingrained these distinctions really are. There was an appalling symbolic dynamic in the Civil

War which almost split the nation in two, before the first centennial. What power was at work there? How do you explain it?

—◆◆◆—

If you live in the East or the West, you live in terms of the dynamic rather than the static. But as we move from East to West we build up behind us the fixity of the past so that from the Western point of view the East seems static indeed, whereas from the point of view of the North or South each seems transient and unstable.

—◆◆◆—

The great center of prestige as far as literature is concerned resides unequivocally in the East. Gary Snyder recently received the Pulitzer Prize, and he was the first Californian poet ever to gain the award.[25] Jeffers never got it; Rexroth never got it; Duncan has yet to get it. Part of the exacerbation of being an artist in the West is the knowledge that the East passes its favors around most selectively, and honors chiefly its own kind.

—◆◆◆—

What is the Western energy? To discover that, you have to go to its symbolic source; for it is always the symbol which is the locus of energy in any creative sense. To get to the core of this, we have to probe back into the power of the negative and analyze just what it is doing in terms of the Western ethos.

—◆◆◆—

The first thing that comes to mind is the sundown area, the West, and the death which is associated with sundown. This is a strange thing because as the energies proceed from East to West, the latter seems to be the focal point of all the expansive energy of the nation. Yet there is always the death factor latent in that energy. When men left the East coast to go to the Western frontier, there was always a kind of creative death which seemed to await them. They had hopes for a new start and a new life, but the fact of death was always around them. They could be destroyed by the titanic scale of the West—the land, the wilderness, the Indians.

—◆◆◆—

This means that there is always an undercurrent of violence latent in the Western archetype. Whenever you get excessiveness in scale you get extreme tension and the possibility of rupture of form. Because the landscape of the West is greater than the individual consciousness, you get an extenuation of the structure and the possibility of collapse and destruction. This is indicated by the size of our states as you move West. Rhode Island is quite small, but as the nation moved West the states got bigger and bigger, until Inyo County in California is larger than Rhode Island. The scale of men's political and commercial lives became stretched, and this stretch becomes a point of tension, sometimes of collapse.

—◆◆◆—

Of course, when you get to the Pacific, there is really no further place to go. If you try Hawaii, you find yourself in the Orient. I've heard it said that the only place an oriental can feel comfortable in the United States is in Hawaii. The Orient begins there, on its new round across the globe. At the Pacific Coast, there is a sense of termination. Look out at the ocean and the whole thing seems to come to a halt, and it's not only a cultural shock but a shock deep in the spirit. It is a mystery, and it is a threat; the soul is revulsed to find itself at the end of the line.

—◆◆◆—

Here we have encountered one of those paradoxes. As an artist, instead of participating in the national expansion to the West, suddenly you have to stop and think of addressing yourself to the East. The alternative is to build up a kind of Western provincialism, and it is easy to fall into. Out here we try to perfect our own cultural forms, our own cultural outlets. We create our literary magazines and our publishing houses. But these are rarely successful and rarely have much impact. Insofar as they remain provincial, they give us outlets, but it is not as if they carried an effective voice. Really to make a contribution to the nation at large, we have to think in different terms. This initially goes against the grain, but soon becomes seductive. When prestige beckons, traditionally the Western artist sells out and goes East.

—◆◆◆—

But the sundown state has its own dreamy, seductive side too. One reason why the drug cult has such a foothold in California is precisely because of that. Never forget that the state flower of California is the poppy.

—◆◆◆—

Out here you can gravitate to places like San Francisco or Los Angeles where life is easy in terms of climate. You find yourself falling into pockets of your own kind where there is no necessity for struggle. You relapse into a flaccid communion with your own fellows via the drug. This is not new, either. Studies of California life in the 1890s show that both the opium and cocaine trades were heavy here. The opium trade from the Orient came right through the Gate, and a lot of it rubbed off.

—◆◆◆—

A low level of institutional life generally means a high level of hedonism and pleasure seeking. The soft climate of the coast and the lethargy of the life leads to a certain abandon here. The California Indians, they say, were some of the least developed primitives in the world because the living here was so easy. The struggle for existence was so minimal that no high-conscious forms of creativity or religious activity needed to be developed, usually the compensation for a rigorous struggle against nature. On the other hand, Kit Carson said the Klamath warriors were tougher than the Blackfeet. A land of paradoxes.

—◆◆◆—

Living in the West, there are things that you have to be wary of as you begin to thread your way through the problems of the creative life. It is also important in the sexual life. The lack of structure in California means that your basic relationships are under a certain erosion before you get started. Almost all commitments have a certain reservation about them—"I love you—if it works out." There is always that *if* in Californian relationships which is deceptive. The search for fullness of life militates against the relationships of life.

—◆◆◆—

I am talking here primarily about the Coast. What I am saying doesn't apply so much to the Interior Valley, the Bible Belt of California where I grew up. I know a guy from Missouri who says that whenever he feels homesick he goes to Turlock.

—◆◆◆—

Yet, by another kind of a paradox, even though California is the sundown state and therefore partakes of the death symbol, Californians as a rule have very little positive relationship towards death at all. In one way, people from around the country come out here to die, but in another way they come here to live forever. Nothing dies in California; it is the land of non-death. After all, California is so new that you can almost say that nothing has died here compared to the rest of the world. There is no intrinsic knowledge in the sense of locality—our graveyards have been built within living memory. This cultural shallowness in terms of the life experience is heady and deceptive.

—◆◆◆—

This also has its allure, however, with a sense of unreality about it. Think of all the novels which have been written about Forest Lawn in Los Angeles. Such conventionalization of death on a very middle-class level is usually taken to mean a refusal to face facts. All those pet graveyards where sums of money have been placed in living perpetuity to dead animals have provided the world with the stereotype of sentimentality.

—◆◆◆—

This is a very mysterious place to be. Strange, excessive energies are released here, but also strange lethargies, pitfalls, and quicksands. Death Valley and Mount Whitney, the highest and lowest points, are so close to each other you can spit from the top of the world to the bottom. Such vast deserts and such high peaks. Such inordinate productivity in the soil of the fertile valleys, yet such terminal points at the edge of the coast. This makes our literature erratic. Western literature tends to be powerful and energetic, but lacking in cohesion. Part of the problem of the artist is to bring cohesion to the sheer power of the creative force piling up in the West. Take it from me, it is hard work.

—◆◆◆—

In my view the greatest writer we have produced is Jeffers.[26] His ability to engage the factor of violence and come to terms with it gives him a centrality no other writer has equaled. He was able to seize the power of the negative and make a positive out of it. He took almost every celebrated California virtue and negated it in everything he wrote, at the same time making it the source of his energies.

—◆◆◆—

154

The unconscious religion in the West is pantheism. Nature seems to carry the whole thrust of the divine. Established religions have a very shallow footing in the West. It is as if the California experience of religion is affective, something entering into you in a physical way. Especially in the coastal region, where there is the great drop-off point and the intensity of the sea, sustained church-going is difficult. Why should we sit in church on a Sunday when God is walking on water out there?

—◆◆—

There is also a profound relationship in the American imagination between the idea of California and the idea of gold. Whatever the allure is in that symbol it is something that I don't really understand. What is the attraction of gold? It seems to be one of the most magnetic symbols in the history of human consciousness, and it is feminine. The element of allure inculcates a profoundly feminine resonance.

—◆◆—

The idea of California as a feminine state is pretty well ingrained in the national consciousness. That quality of allure and glamour which men associate with femininity seems to be localized in the California image. The beauty of the state is feminine. When you read someone like Edmund Wilson, who lived in the patriarchal East, writing about California, you sense a fear of the feminine as he describes the lassitude out here. It is as if man's critical consciousness, too long associated with California, would become supine and inert, content merely with indulgence. When Henry James visited California in 1905, he was shaken by the natural beauty of the State but contemptuous of Californian cultural pretensions. That beauty he saw as feminine, but of purposive masculine civilization he found nothing at all.

—◆◆—

Yet the energies of the frontier are essentially associated with masculine aggressiveness. You see some of the explosive ingredients which are latent in the symbolism of the West. It's a dangerous mixture, believe me. I know, because I, too, am its mouthpiece.

—◆◆◆—

In the late Fifties, there were forty thousand people a week coming to California. Forty thousand a week! A new city every seven days! By 1962 we had the largest population of any state. Now they are going back again, disillusioned, turning around to the midwest, the south, the north. Yet other hopefuls keep coming. In Oregon, people are worried the same thing might happen there. Their bumper stickers read, "Don't Californicate Oregon." What kind of an image is that? The harlot of the West.

—◆◆◆—

Outside, the sun is going down. The month of May has peaked and is moving towards June. Summer is over the horizon. All the fields are almost excessively luxuriant in the late rains. I have never seen the wild flowers so profuse and enchanting. The wild lilac is simply spectacular. Such a surfeit of blessings—why should anyone struggle?

—◆◆◆—

What happens to the work-ethic when it strains its muscle to come West and then hits this? What a tremendous taking of wind from the sails. To arrive out here with no place to expend the energy. The disintegration of California artists is awesome. You can hardly get started in one direction and there is a tapering off. There is a constantly shifting focus. What are you going to do? Lie in the grass or swim in the ocean? Climb a mountain or surf in the sea? Pass out or run crazy? The problem of direction—when you hit the end-stop where do you go? When all the impulsion is from East to West and suddenly there is no more West, it is as if the

156

vibration of the tuning fork just hangs in there and won't quit.

—◆◆◆—

Somehow, all these liabilities are subsumed in my own life. In many ways, my whole life has been the challenge of pulling them together, making them coherent. Certainly my work has been that, but also my life. I've tried to learn how to change those liabilities to assets, from the negative to the positive. It really takes some doing, and whether you are committed to a life of work or to a life of leisure, you are not going to get through it scot-free. The only way you can do it is through direct experience, through your pain and your anguish. It will depend on your capacity to rise from your wounds, although you will have no patterns to go by. As soon as there seems to be a pattern it will be shot down because the anti-pattern forces are stronger here than the pattern forces. The secret of living in this state of extreme flux, of fear and trembling, simply to withstand the demands on the imagination, is a difficult thing to find. The scale of the imagination is such, however, that once you make it comprehensive within yourself a solution is discovered which will work for both you and the race. The whole world looks to this point; it can do no other. The West always will be the end of the line, the end-stop, as long as there is a sun which goes from East to West. To master the art of existence in California is to master it for the world. The witness that awaits you is that impressive.

Meditation Fifteen: Regionalism

In this meditation I want to move into regionalism itself, probing whatever there is about it that will come to terms with its potency. Perhaps a good place to begin is the spirit of place, which, of course, immediately conjures up implications of D. H. Lawrence. He never wrote a book about it, at least none with that title. But Richard Aldington published a selection of Lawrence's work which groups the regional emphasis under that subtitle.[27] Ever since, we have associated the phrase with his name.

—◆◆◆—

Wherever he went, Lawrence tried to discern the particular spirit of the place in which he found himself. He did this with great perceptiveness, and it occurs to me that, as far as the regional emphasis goes, it is perhaps the chief part of his witness. Whereas true regionalists like Frost and Jeffers and Steinbeck and Faulkner spoke always in terms of identification as the key element, Lawrence did not. He smelled out the spirit of place everywhere he went. But it would be hard to say that he identified anywhere with that spirit as a locale.

—◆◆◆—

Thus, I've always found it curious that Lawrence was such a restless soul. He was tempted by a few core places such as New Mexico, but his personal relationships were always intruding upon that situational sense. His attempt to find a

159

unity based on regionalism was always doomed to failure, not because of the region but because the local community (and his own nerves) couldn't permit him such sustained relationships. This was especially true of women. He attracted women to him, but their attachment was always a kind of exacerbation for him. Moreover he was always trying to find the perfect masculine relationship, which he never found either, so he was condemned to wander. He was always looking for the spirit of place as a clue to where his earthly quest was to be resolved. Tragically, he never found it.

—◆◆—

I suppose that the psychological basis for the spirit of place goes back to the maternal—we speak of the *mother country*, the *mother land*. As we will see later there is a definite physiological basis to it, but in psychology it is called the *participation mystique*. It is built upon a connatural relationship between the sensitive person and the area with which he identifies.

—◆◆—

This can be very powerful sometimes, so powerful as to become a limitation, not allowing the artist to deepen into the realm of the universal. A modernist scorn of regionalist painting has to do with what is called *local color.* Often you will hear a critic dismiss a work as being nothing more than local color. Of course, that is always a temptation for an intelligence which, unable to grasp the universal inferences, is content to simply register the oddities and eccentricities of a given region. But the ultimate energies, no matter how local, always lie in the universal.

—◆◆—

Local color, however, is not the essence of regionalism, which is a centering device, a way of getting to a higher state of being, participation in a greater frame of reference.

Conversely, regionalism forms a conduit back so that the substance of the greater frame may return to the individual. This is its real secret—not merely what you put into the landscape, but what the landscape puts into you.

—◆◆◆—

The efflux back into you is based on a reality greater than the natural fact itself. Until you are able to reach through the membrane of nature to the abstract principle beyond, you will not be successful. The medium, which is in this case the landscape, becomes intense with both the power of the world of the subjective beholder and the greater abstract world which lies beyond. This sense of a mediation point between the two realities is at the heart of what regionalism really is.

—◆◆◆—

Almost always in authentic regionalism, there are certain pronounced physical characteristics in the landscape which are determining factors. These characteristics serve the hierophantic function, as they are sources of the great mystery which lies beyond. Cities also have a way of doing this. You tend to identify with your city, which is a maternal symbol. The mother-city, the mother-region, the motherland. Indeed, this can be cynically exploited, as in the case of sports. One year you go out and root for the home team, and the next year all the players are sold to other cities, but you return to root for the "new" home team again. This doesn't mean, however, that the *fact* of participation in the local isn't valuable in itself. For one thing we do have to find is some way to break up the tyranny of the technological world as laid across the whole of human life. The atomization of the family and all social relationships within the great flux of commerce and technology has got to be stemmed. One of the central ways of doing this is through the regional emphasis, especially in the arts.

—◆◆◆—

The very idea behind the word regionalism has a geographical base, but often that supposed geography is really a city which has little geographical singularity about it. Yet, it constellates space in a certain way so that the adhesion, the *participation mystique,* develops around the city itself. Where I grew up, in Fresno County, the identification was north with San Francisco, whereas in Tulare County, the next county south, everyone looked to Los Angeles. This prejudice was so deep you wouldn't believe it. In my home town[28] farmers wore little pouches on their belts to carry their silver dollars. When paper money came into use during the Twenties they were suspicious of it. It was insubstantial and ephemeral to them. They called it "L. A. money."

—◆◆—

Yet, even though San Francisco dominated the cultural situation clear down to Fresno, when I came to write, it wasn't of the city at all, but of the Valley itself. My identification with that area was so profound that it became in the end a threat to my continued development. Once you identify so fully with the local scene, it takes great resilience of mind somehow to probe through to the universal factor. As it turned out, the fates of my life took me out of there. And it was the direct movement of that loss that broke up the *participation mystique* and set me free. Yet the poetry remains valid because the religious element, the universal, transcended the merely local. When I returned to California, it was to the Bay Area; the Bay became the central factor around which the new regionalism began to develop, and San Francisco was the hub of it. You see this creative tension between city and surroundings. The city of Fresno simply did not have the cultural and symbolic force to accomplish that earlier. The great stretch of the San Joaquin utterly overwhelmed it.

—◆◆—

The Bay. Mt. Tamalpais on the North, Mt. Diablo on the East, great bodies of water and open vistas in between. The run-off of the whole central Sierra drains out through Carquinas Strait and the Golden Gate. Every time you step out of your house, no matter where you are around the area, somehow the presence of the Bay is always there. Man's work on it, the great slender bridges that span those waters, is incredible. It's a marvelous, beautiful, powerfully compelling place. You can create almost endlessly out of its materials; they are that rich.

—◆◆◆—

One of the problems with Los Angeles is that it lacks geographical center. It sprawls on a sort of shelf on the coast under a bland climate, although its desert landscape is compelling. Yet Los Angeles lacks the hub-center of San Francisco, and will probably never be the city of in-depth creativity that San Francisco is. However, there are certain rewards in living there. The life style is relaxed and more out of doors than to the north. If you crave anonymity it will hide you. In fact, if you want to sin, go to Los Angeles—no one will ever know you are there. In San Francisco, on the other hand, you may well run into any friend downtown on weekends.

—◆◆◆—

When I was a lad in the C.C.C. we used to go down to the Valley towns on Saturday night.[29] I remember an Irishman named Mullins and how delighted he was to be able to raise hell where no one knew him. To me San Francisco at that time was a vast, terrifying anonymity of a metropolis, but to him every street was Main. Actually, that's the latent maternal archetype in the city. No matter into what hole he crawled there was always his mother shaking her finger at him.

—◆◆◆—

So. What do we have? The local, the regional, the sectional, the national, and the universal. In every work of art there are the several levels of culture, all of which should be incorporated. Every great writer has somehow to produce out of each one of those levels. *The Modernist era is over.* Once again it is the viability of local materials and local ways of seeing through things to the factors of existence beyond them. We are again responding to direct emotional values, rather than abstract and intellectual ones. We are beginning to wake up.

—◆◆◆—

Any new religious movement that is going to arise will inevitably be based on the regional aspect. Even in the case of a universal religion such as Catholicism, it must develop regional accents that are derived from the spirit of place if it is to remain viable.

—◆◆◆—

The two greatest American regional poets to emerge in the twentieth century are Frost and Jeffers. Frost found himself in New England, Jeffers on the Big Sur. To me, it is significant that both of those are rocky, restrictive landscapes. The stony fields of New England gave Frost his integral character, and the sharp, jagged cliffs of Big Sur gave Jeffers his power. The force of the integer resides in all regionalism, and you have to seek it out somehow.

—◆◆◆—

I once made the statement that the problem of living in the Big Sur was that the spectacular beauty of the place has a way of searching out the flaw in a man. Too often he breaks up on the rocks. Kerouac made his own book of interior chaos and called it *Big Sur*.[30] Of course, the thesis is straight out of Jeffers. To him, extreme landscapes have a way of provoking extremities in individual psyches. Whatever the flaw is, it will be searched out by the extremity; sooner or later that flaw will manifest itself in the life. Then the drama will be enacted around that flaw amidst the grandeur of the landscape. To live in the Sur, you had better be ready to cope with the negative capability within yourself because you are going to be put to the test.

—◆◆◆—

Another great source of the power of regionalism is its immediacy. When you begin writing, one of the first things you should do is make the weft and fabric of what you create from the basic responses to that which is around you. You have to get beyond this eventually, but always you have to begin in terms of it. The problem is first to build the base, then transcend the base which you have established. That is the principle out of which every significant work of art is achieved.

—◆◆◆—

The region is not so much man's relation to God, as God's relation to man. It is the force through which God participates in the whole. Some writers on regionalism have spoken of it as the problem of the atman and the brahman, or the soul and God. If wholeness in your individual life comes through participation in the greater whole of the cosmos, then the regional factor is going to have to take a strong place. If you can find your region and develop your regional proclivities, a great deal of the problem of the abstractness of life is going to be solved for you. If you can make of it a strong archetypal configuration it will have universal appeal. Take Mt. Shasta, for example. How many communes are located around it today? Dozens. There is something about that mountain which takes you out of yourself and relates you to the whole. At the same time, the mountain also puts something back into you, and this is why they call it the solution to the atman and the brahman equation. The mountain acts as a transcendent symbol because it is a medial one.

—◆◆◆—

You must think about regionalism in terms of your own life. Do you go where you belong, and then start from there? Or do you go where the opportunities *seem* to be, and cut yourself off from your roots? Often you will find that your greatest strengths come not from being where the opportunities are, but from where you belong. Many times, when you follow the opportunities, you lose your capabilities. Sometimes, of course, you have no choice, you are torn from your place, but then you must be strong enough to cope. In my case, I was tested by my region before I had to meet the ordeal of the world. In some way, I had managed to encompass the region in my work so that I could graduate beyond it and survive, even though up to that point I had declared it to be the great sustaining element in my life. At the time, I had no wish to move on to any other place, but as I look back on it now I can see that it was a godsend that I was taken out of the Valley. I would never have moved of my own volition.

—✦✦✦—

Participation in the greater whole. That is the archetype working behind regionalism. If you have both a good city and a beautiful region, and recognize them as such and identify with them, many problems of life will be solved for you right there. But first you have to recognize those forces, and then trust them.

—✦✦✦—

As in the case of Big Sur, sometimes the region can be excessive. San Francisco is the suicide capital of the world, and it is almost as if the Golden Gate Bridge is the symbol of that, the vibration line between here and eternity. They always jump off on the inside, however, never the seaward side. It is the maternal element drawing them back. The devouring womb.

—✦✦✦—

166

It goes without saying that the whole problem of regionalism in America boils down to the ineluctable distance between nature and man. Remember Auden's comment that for the American, nature is a beautiful virgin who has to be taken by force? This is changing, but you can't build communes around Shasta without in some way suffering a terrible reproof from the goddess you are propiating. I think all cities are built to save men from the accusation of nature. Jeffers founded his whole philosophy on the idea that men have turned their faces away from nature; they have sealed themselves in cities so that the face of God is closed to them. He carried that sense of an austere break between man and nature to a more extreme pitch than anyone had ever done before, and it is significant that it took a Californian to do it. It is almost as if it were the apotheosis of an underlying American archetype. We had to get out here to reach that point of totality.

—◆◆◆—

Sometimes, out here, you go to one of those beach houses built on an incredible cove with the crashing sea confronting you through the picture window. It takes a lot of guts to face a thing of beauty like that, day in and day out. You really have to have it together. There is an incredible amount of psychic force generated on a strip of coast, and if you try to shut it out it finds ways of circling back into your mind. Your dreams will tell you. Yet, if you spend your time extolling it, nothing else gets done. You must honor your region, but you must find places to live in it that are suitable for the survival of your human spirit. The confrontation element really is terrific, and you just can't put yourself in a situation where every day you are tested by a thing like the coast or Mount Shasta. Don't underestimate the regional archetype. It can literally drive you mad.

—◆◆◆—

I once heard an architect say that you should never build with a picture window facing a beautiful view. It inures your mind in the end, deadens it with the glaze of distraction. Settle *near* a view if you must, he said, but not *before* one. In that way, every time you step around the bend you get a fresh perspective. If you have to look at it all the time, day in and day out, you start denying the most powerful things in your life because they become too much for you. Never forget a home is first of all a shelter. Leave the big picture windows to the foolhardy. The real estate people say those big spreads have a turnover rate of two or three years.

—◆◆◆—

We live in a triumphant civilization, and we tend to start from a position of collective strength. If you've got the money, we say, then build the house. Pick out the best place you can find, buy the ground, and you've got it made, man. Why not? Why not, indeed! Buying land is like buying a woman—you just *think* you've bought her.

—◆◆◆—

Be very wary of beauty. The greatest beauty is the beauty of God, and He didn't put you into this life merely to amuse yourself. He exacts back every ounce of consciousness he has endowed you with. Participation in a greater life. Find your place, and learn to listen to the spirit of that place. Learn to let it come into you in subtle ways. Make pilgrimages to the great natural artifacts. Go to Shasta. Go to Yosemite. Go to the Grand Canyon. But remember, don't gorge at the trough. Don't be a glutton.

—◆◆◆—

I think this is proved by the works of Jeffers himself. In the end the Sur did wreak its imposition on his mind. In the end it did dictate its values, rigidify his thought. He remained true to its vibration, and that is to his credit. But he failed to penetrate beyond its implications, and that is not. Let us say simply that he got too close to it. He succumbed to its allure, and it exacted of him the ultimate fee: possession.

—◆◆◆—

But learn to contemplate the spirit of place wherever you go. Think first of all, what is this spirit? What does it mean to me in my stay here? Try to think of the events which happen to you as a reflection from that spirit of place. It is the medium through which the greater whole is manifesting itself to you.

Meditation Sixteen: Landscape and Eros

In the attempt to understand the significance of re-
gionalism recent writers have tended to divide into two
approaches, the phenomenological and the symbolic. Next
time we will be meditating on the latter, under the heading
"Sacred Space," but today it is region under what might be
called its biological aspect that is our subject. * We might call
this meditation "Landscape and Eros," the relation between
situation and libido, or rather the relation of libido to the
all-encompassing presence of place.

—◆◆◆—

Put in these terms landscape and eros do not seem so
strange a conjunction as at first appeared. We have already
spoken of the intense vibration that landscape impresses on
the deep subjectivity, stimulating and invigorating. It can't
be all that astonishing, then, if, among all the stimuli,
libido would also be aroused. Certainly beauty, beauty
alone, has an intense reaction upon libido. As a youth, I was
brought to a distinct sexual heat by the exaltation and mag-

---

*Parts of this meditation and the following one were incorporated
in the essay "The Regional Incentive." See the author's *Earth
Poetry: Selected Essays & Interviews, 1950–1977* (Berkeley:
Oyez, 1980), p. 195.

nitude of California scenery. Sometimes that came from the fruitfulness of the farmlands at midsummer, but at other times I could trace it to the contour of landscape itself. I remember once when I was in the Order, no longer a youth but a grown man in my forties, on an outing near Mission San Jose we chanced on a landscape that stopped me in my tracks, like an encounter with a woman. The nude sunburnt hills lay undulant as a supine giantess, somnolent in repose. I felt I could enter the cleavage between those breasts, sink down on that belly, become enfolded in those encompassing thighs, and lose myself forever. Of course I do not discount the part played by celibacy in that uprush of feeling, for it is undeniable. Incarcerated from women during the war I found a mere forked tree intolerable to behold, almost seeing the pubic hair in the crotch. The lumberjacks call such trees "schoolmarms." They don't need a psychologist to tell them what's in their minds.

—◆◆◆—

So you see, even before we're well launched we've already turned up enough correspondences between landscape and eros to establish the connection. In this meditation, though, I want to approach it from another point of view. Let me read to you a passage from Paul Shepard's *Man in the Landscape* which opened up new perspectives for me. He writes:

> In man territoriality is an intricate association of tenderness and antipathy, in which both are closely related to the terrain. In him too the territorial instinct varies greatly according to circumstances. It is the household, property in land, the tribal range. Perhaps even the city, state, and nation are meta-territories. The attention which the individual gives to the territory is related to his age and perhaps the season. Alaskan wolves do not seem to recognize territorial bounds or even the context of territorialism, until they reach breeding age, whereupon they mate for life, learn the territorial

bounds, and join in to defend it. In some primitive human groups ties between puberty and the right to hunt hint at a similar relation between age and perception of the landscape; indeed, the major role of the territory is perpetuation of a reproductive unit. Territorial establishment and maintenance is closely related to sexuality and to other socializing processes. For love of another is linked to love of place.[31]

Thus the technological age, with its scorn of nature and its dehumanization of art, has produced the highest divorce rate in human history. Because men and women can no longer identify with a place, they can scarcely identify with each other.

—◆◆◆—

"Love of another is linked to love of place." It is this ineluctable mystery that I wish to dwell on today. First of all, it seems to me such a beautiful idea, so redemptive and healing. I mean, the thrust of contemporary sexology—the new science of sexology—is so reductive and divisive that it seems bent on destroying the essence of sex in order to achieve its demythologization. It is preoccupied with dispassionate analysis, separating male from female, organ from organ, sensation from sensation. It is as if sex exists in a vacuum, functioning at a remove from the rest of life. It is as if we have separated it essentially from ourselves. Certainly we have separated it from the family, the nuclear family. Many of you, perhaps most of you, are living together outside of marriage, as a matter of course. There's nothing new about premarital sex, assuredly, but somehow I get the sense of an avid sexual experimentation among you, as of something almost dictated by a current trend, a state of mind. It is against such a compulsion that the phrase "love of another is linked to love of place" has its shock value. It stops the clock.

—◆◆◆—

My hunch is that the abrupt shift such a reminder causes points up the distinction between sexuality and *mating*. Mating is the activity through which sexuality is confirmed in positive identification. Unquestionably centered on sexuality, it is nevertheless the norm by which sexuality is accommodated into social life. That it is something even more is suggested by its relation to territorial imperatives, and hence to landscape. Shepard continues:

> This awareness of the territory at mating suggests imprinting, an irreversible learning at a critical period in the individual's life, attaching significant and inherent meaning to an appropriate yet fortuitous object. It is part of the normal development of all young animals, a predisposition at a certain age to learn certain things which cannot thereafter be easily unlearned. It is the ultimate *idée fixe*. Young crows, for example, fixate on their parent crows or whoever is tending them at an age of seventeen days. If they fixate on people instead of crows at that time they become much tamer and more docile. In men such processes probably involve the indelible memories of childhood. There may be types of human imprinting which we do not know to occur amongst other creatures, such as fixation on dream images, on art forms, or on architecture . . .[32]

And, of course, as he had already suggested, on landscape.

—◆◆◆—

Without doubt, for me the regional awareness had indeed been one of the indelible memories of childhood. However, it became conscious only in my dual awakening, the encounter with woman confirmed in early manhood by the dawn of my vocation as poet. When I became a poet, woman and religion fused together in an ineluctable synthesis that constituted what I can only call an entirely new identity, an unprecedented sense of my own self awareness. Not only did I see myself in human terms as a native of the San Joaquin, but in religious terms I saw myself as the predestined voice of that region, its prophet. These coalesced together in my love of a woman and my love of the land, and with increasing maturity achieved a definite ambience, a distinct sense of equipoise and grace.

FEAST DAY

Peace was the promise: this house in the vineyard,
Under the height of the great tree
Loosing its leaves on the autumn air.
East lie the mountains;
Level and smooth lie the fields of vines.

Now on this day in the slope of the year,
Over the wine and the sheaf of grain,
We shape our hands to the sign, the symbol,
Aware of the room, the sun in the sky,
The earnest immaculate rhythm of our blood,
As two will face in the running light,
Ritual born of the heavy season,
And see suddenly on all sides reality,
Vivid again through the crust of indifference,
Waken under the eye.

East lie the mountains,
Around us the level length of the earth;
And this house in the vines,
Our best year,
Golden grain and golden wine,
In autumn, the good year falling south.[33]

Here the erotic and religious conjoin to complete the regional mandala that is the soul's orientation point in reality.

—◆◆—

Undoubtedly this same synthesis obtained in the ordeal of vocation of Robinson Jeffers. Although he found both his vocation and his woman before he discovered his region, it was the belated arrival in his life of the latter, the Big Sur

175

coast, which transmuted him into the darkly brooding and transcendent figure that confirmed his unique self-finding. In fact he indicated as much in the foreword to his *Selected Poetry* when he juxtaposed the untamed spirit of his woman and the untamed spirit of his region as the explosive ingredients that lit him to incandescence.[34] Jeffers maintained his identity with the region of his self-finding until the end of his life, as he maintained his identity with his wife Una long after the close of her own. It was the conjunction in his mind of these two images that gave him the continuity of purpose which constitutes the essence of his achievement.

—◆◆◆—

For me, however, fate had another pattern to enact, and I will instance it here in order to show how much these two strains, the sexual and the sacred, are bound together to make up the magic of the regional archetype. The poem "Feast Day," which I just read, was written on Thanksgiving Day of 1939, right after the opening of World War II in Europe. In the poem the sense of erotic identification and regional equipoise is manifest, but within three years that selfsame war had thrown us apart, never to take up life in the Valley again. The dual myth of woman and region was shattered in the appalling crisis of separation, and neither of us ever returned. It was the most devastating thing that ever happened to me, and the depotentiation of the numen invested in the region never survived the going of the girl.

—◆◆◆—

It is true I have remained a regionalist in the broader, California sense. Later I identified with the San Francisco Bay area in the Forties and Fifties, and have recently put down roots here in the Santa Cruz mountains. It is also true that these Californian, San Franciscan, and now Santa Cruzan identities have been maintained and confirmed by the women I have loved, who have given my life its discernible contour. But never again has the "imprint" taken as it did in that first awakening when the eros of woman and region conjoined to make me a lover and a celebrator of life, who stood forth in his sexual identity as well as in his sacred space, and, gathering about him the vastness of the world in which he was born, opened his throat and praised his God.

—◆◆◆—

You can see from this how mating centers and lends coherence to the inveterate indiscriminateness of sexuality, its remorseless disregard of persons and communal values, its inflexible verge toward pure function. But it also shows how mating itself is not simply a pairing, but is centered on broader determinants, of which territory is the reproductive context, and landscape the aesthetic one. This, of course, is not the whole of it. Animals mate; mankind alone marries. And it is only in marriage that the values consequent upon personality are fostered and consummated. You might say we *recognize* our mate, whereas marriage is a *choice*. But mating must be there, essential to marriage, giving biological substance to the recognition that makes choice inevitable.

—◆◆◆—

So today in your living together some of you are simply paired, nothing more. It will end tomorrow. Others of you are indeed mated, but not yet married, as myself, back in my own youth in the Valley, was long mated before I chose to marry. I know now it was the Valley itself that induced the mating, provided the mysterious context within which mating is consummated. But that was not complete until another dimension, not dependent on the regional imperative that plays so potent a role in mating, provided the compact in which two spirits, their mating proved through long association, at last acknowledged the sovereignty of choice.

—◆◆◆—

Traditionally, as lived by the race in its long history, and as validated by religion, the human family has evolved along a certain line of coherence. First there is mating, which is recognition; next there is marriage, which is choice; then sexuality, which is consummation, the dynamic in which recognition and choice are realized. Finally there is sacrament, the infusion of God into the procreation of men and women. This synthesis our age has shattered, pitching us abruptly into sexuality without either recognition or choice, and jettisoning sacrament. I believe this is principally because we have lost the sense in our lives of the primacy of place, the magic circle in which mating is achieved.

——◆◆◆——

For it is mating which is the underlying mystery, and sacrament, the upper mystery which crowns it. Marriage we know. We grasp its contractual element and its precepts and its obligations. All are spelled out. Sexuality we know: we know its term, which is procreation, and its beginning, which is eros. But mating and sacrament, these we do not know. One is a mystery of nature, and the other is a mystery of God. It is as if the infra-rational and the supra-rational conspired to confound us, in order to elevate us out of ourselves.

——◆◆◆——

For is there a stranger power than mating? That awesome chemistry by which a man and a woman recognize each other, and seek each other out confounding family, friends, nationality, religion? Whole empires are shattered as Antony and Cleopatra rush into each other's arms. History is pockmarked with the craters left by the explosions of lovers when their paths cross and recognition ensues. There is no power in this life that can be compared to it.

——◆◆◆——

178

Sacrament, too, is mystery. All sacraments are divine ordinances calculated to reinforce human life at its key points of transformation. The strange thing to me about the sacrament of matrimony is its position, its final place in the marital sequence, following rather than preceding procreation. After all, two people have mated; they have recognized each other. In their social contract they have decisively chosen. Is it not enough for God? You would think He would be glad to say, "Go forth now, my children, be fruitful and multiply." No way. Only after consummation, only after the direct physical fulfillment, only after the phallus splits the hymen and kisses the womb, does God bow and bless. The whole ritual of the marriage ceremony can be enacted but until it actually happens in bed there is no sacrament. Surely there lies the wonder and the mystery. It is only in bed that mating and sacrament are confirmed in sexuality.

—◆◆◆—

This penchant of God for such strange reservations sometimes puts religion, as an institution, in a difficult place. An unconsummated marriage is no marriage at all, but how do you prove it? Occasionally a couple will come pleading back to the priest seeking annulment on the grounds of nonconsummation. How can they prove it? If they can be shown through witnesses to have never been alone together the Church will agree. But even if the couple were alone for the briefest time She cannot yield. More than one marriage has been consummated in some broom closet between the altar and the sacristy, with the bride's maid standing guard! "Petticoats up and trousers down." The power of mating. The terrible splendor of sexuality.

—◆◆◆—

No wonder it takes a sacrament to seal mating around with divine strengths. No wonder it takes all the power of place to support the magnificent passion and splendor of sex. Eros and landscape. That, I suppose, is what this meditation has done for me—made mating more comprehensible in the aura of the spirit of place, the magic ring in which two souls recognize each other, then in decisive choice enact physical consummation as the mystery of eros finds its locus in the mystery of place.

Meditation Seventeen: Sacred Space

Now the term is drawing to a close. Springtime has run its course and full summer is upon us. The heat holds firm. Out across the canyons the hills are golden to the sea. From up here the sea itself is flat as blue slate. Everywhere the light falls, without diminution and seemingly without end. The year climbs toward solstice and bears us with it.

—◆◆◆—

When I look into your faces I am struck by the differences I see from when you began last autumn. It is not a difference that nine months acquisition of knowledge has wrought. It is the difference between fall and summer. You arrived late in September with your faces expectant and resolute, throwing yourself into the work awaiting you, eager to make your mark on the unknown, to make a dent in your ignorance and fill it with a little knowledge. Now all that is over. Your faces register a profound shift in inner disposition. There is a fullness as of summer about you. You eye each other with a strange urgency to be gone, almost a yearning. Like the summer itself, you seek consummation.

—◆◆◆—

One of the deepest needs of the human soul is for a center, a focus which confers meaning on the shapelessness of temporal existence. Perhaps the most basic, after the awareness

181

of family, is man's apprehension of his immediate locale. For the surrounding landscape represents something markedly other—indeed the eternal presence of Otherness— and as such it carries the vibration of divinity. In man's identification with his region he realizes what he is by intuiting everything he is not. Close at hand and yet aloofly apart, it stands as the mandala of his unconscious associations, one of the ineradicable patterns of psychic life. As such, the recourse to landscape in the need for coherence has from time immemorial elevated man to his most profound religious intuitions. Mountains, valley, rivers, islands. Always he has looked to the configuration of the world about him for the Face of God.

—◆◆◆—

We are familiar with the idea of a break-in-plane as it refers to time—the archetypal tension between linear and cyclical time. Here we approach the break-in-plane as it applies to space, the tension between sacred and profane space. It becomes the fundamental way of organizing relative value in the encompassing environment.

—◆◆◆—

In his book *The Sacred and the Profane*, Mircea Eliade, the historian of religion, addresses himself directly to the break inherent in space itself. "For religious man," he writes, "space is not homogeneous . . . some parts of space are qualitatively different from others." And he goes on:

> It must be said at once that the religious experience of the nonhomogeneity of space is a primordial experience, [equivalent] to a founding of the world. It is not a matter of theoretical speculation, but a primary religious experience that precedes all reflection on the world. For it is the break effected in space that allows the world to be constituted, because it reveals the fixed point, the central axis for all future orientation. When the sacred manifests itself in any hierophany, there is also revelation of an absolute reality,

opposed to the nonreality of the vast surrounding expanse. The manifestation of the sacred ontologically founds the world. In the homogeneous and infinite expanse, in which no point of reference is possible and hence no *orientation* can be established, the hierophany reveals an absolute fixed point, a center.[35]

Eliade goes on to explain that it is for this reason that religious man has always sought to fix his abode at "the center of the world." If the world is to be lived in it must be founded. The discovery of a fixed point or center is equivalent to the creation of the world.

—◆◆◆—

Here we are very close to the idea of the world navel, or *axis mundi*. You remember that in Campbell's monomyth of the hero, the completion of the adventure resulted in the unlocking and release again of the flow of life into the body of the world, the term of all charismatic vocation. What Eliade is showing us just now is that the hero's end was actually his beginning. It begins to look as if his heroic ordeal is simply to transmute his beginning *into* his end. If this is true, consider how important a sense of place is to the fulfillment of charismatic vocation.

—◆◆◆—

Landscape as a centering. The recognition of region as a founding of the world.

—◆◆◆—

In this meditation I want to ponder for a moment the implicit correspondence discernible in the above equation. I mean the correspondence between founding and finding. In the recognition of a sacred space you are founding your world, endowing existence with significance. And in your recognition of vocation you are finding your purpose in life. There it is; the significance of reality is recognition, the purpose of existence is fulfillment. It is so simple it seems simplistic. But in spiritual matters simplicity is of the essence. Simplicity is the guarantor of truth, the token that what is received is permanent and not temporal, substantive and not illusionary.

—◆◆◆—

It is not my purpose here to relate those distinct spiritual moments, the founding and the finding, too inextricably together. Very likely they seldom occur simultaneously. But what relates them is their inherent correspondence, even if several years of linear time separate their moments. Certainly it is possible to find your vocation without founding your world in the sense Eliade means it. But in that case one must insist that the process is not complete. If we can sense their identity then we can say that one without the other is somehow deficient, that the religious element in vocation is not fully liberated into recognition. In such a case almost certainly it lacks grounding. It is not supported by the authority of sacred space.

—◆◆◆—

For the lack of center in the field of space denotes a certain disconnection with the cosmic forces, the pulsating heart of the cosmos itself. Many writers resist this connection. Addressing themselves to the secular milieu as audience they are reluctant to speak in terms they fear are essentially mystical and religious. Ken Kesey in his *Sometimes a Great Notion* is obviously connected to his region in a powerful archetypal way, but he resists the transcendental aspects inherent in the connection. He fights shy, and throws himself back on a brute frontier positivism, a blunt "nothing but" point of view. He has found his vocation and stands in what should be his sacred space, but he refuses to recognize or acknowledge it. He maintains his relation to his secular audience but loses the authority of his prophetic mission.

—◆◆◆—

Steinbeck did the same thing. Growing up under the shadow of Jeffers, as a novelist he settled for a less ambitious option. He founded his region and laid claim on the Salinas Valley to a degree that has never been disputed. But the claim proved too much. Because he did not press forward to the full implications of that founding, he spun sideways, and deflected to New York, where, ensconced in his publisher's office, he wrote little further of significance. The results were predictable in a falling off of creative energy. His best work remains the work of his founding and finding. But denying its implications he succumbed to temptation and sank into mediocrity.

—◆◆◆—

I know many of you do not aspire to be regionalist writers, but you don't have to be a regionalist in order to possess your region. I mean Hardy was a regionalist but his greatest work, *The Dynasts,* was not a regional one. It is an historical epic of the Napoleonic wars, of pronounced national ethos, but his beloved Wessex found little place in it. Nonetheless the transcendent character of the work is manifest. For me it certifies that in founding his region he penetrated into the cosmic source, and entered its life stream. He was an avowed atheist, but in that work his cosmic centeredness is manifest. As far as attribution goes he was a victim of the Newtonian consensus of his time, the Pre-Einsteinian world view. But because his base was founded on archetypal realities, the identity between creativity and space, his work subsumes the energy his thesis denies. Thus we see it is better for a writer to ground himself on symbolic wholes, such as the regional sense of sacred space. Then his ideology can attribute as it pleases.

—◆◆◆—

The founding of the world, the sacred center that renders meaning to the cosmos. Of all the regionalist writers I sense that most strongly in Jeffers. Frost was like Hardy, restricted by the same atheistic attribution, but his regionalism, because archetypally centered, was powerful and operative. With Jeffers this is not so. Although he inherited the same Newtonian scientific purview, his religious pantheism spanned the attributive gap, and released the energies to make a truly sacred space, defined and extolled. Eliot is usually considered the foremost religious poet in English in this century because his *Four Quartets* are solemn, profound, deeply pious, and philosophically astute. But because he makes no recourse to sacred space he cannot unleash the phenomenal energy nor the exalted rapture before the face of God in nature, which is the hallmark of Jeffers.

—◆◆◆—

If the comparison of Eliot to Jeffers is too extreme, compare him to Yeats and see the difference the spirit of place can make in a writer. It is his centering in the sacred space of Ireland that gives Yeats the reach to pass Eliot in verbal power and emotional coherence. Both Eliot and Pound, expatriates each, dangerously severed their American roots, and never recovered the cohesive force that primary identification with sacred space ensures. They are both brilliant, but are basically deficient in emotional location, a lack of a founded world that the great regionalists possess, willful as they sometimes are. Yeats and Jeffers are much closer together, but for an insight into the difference between Californian and Celtic sensibilities read Jeffers' *Descent to the Dead*, poems written on his first visit to Ireland. The Californian violence simply shatters the quiet Celtic twilight. Listen to this one, a poem called "Antrim," written on the Irish coast where it lies closest to Scotland:

No spot on earth where men have so fiercely for ages of time
Fought and survived and cancelled each other,
Pict and Gael and Dane, McQuillan, Clandonnel, O'Neill,
Savages, the Scot, the Norman, the English,
Here in the narrow passage and the pitiless north, perpetual
Betrayals, relentless resultless fighting.

A random fury of dirks in the dark: a struggle for survival
Of hungry blind cells of life in the womb.
But now the womb has grown old, her strength has gone
      forth; a few red carts in a fog creak flax to the dubs,
And sheep in the high heather cry hungrily that life is hard;
      a plaintive peace; shepherds and peasants.

We have felt the blades meet in the flesh in a hundred
      ambushes
And the groaning blood bubble in the throat;
In a hundred battles the heavy axes bite the deep bone,
The mountain suddenly stagger and be darkened.
Generation on generation we have seen the blood of boys
And heard the moaning of women massacred,
The passionate flesh and nerves have flamed like pitch-pine
      and fallen
And lain in the earth softly dissolving.
I have lain and been humbled in all these graves, and mixed
      new flesh with old and filled the hollow of my mouth
With maggots and rotten dust and ages of repose. I lie here
      and plot the agony of resurrection.[36]

It is as if the sacred space of Ireland and Big Sur combined to
found the vortex of violational power.

—◆◆◆—

Where Eliot is superior is his recognition of the sacrality of
personality, and one has the sense that it was this recogni-
tion in his conversion to Christianity that gave him the
only sense of a founded world he knew. This Jeffers denied,
his greatest philosophical and religious weakness. His
rigorous pursuit of objectivity in the science lab at U.S.C.
indoctrinated him thoroughly in the distrust of subjective
anthropomorphism. After that his disgust of human mo-
tives was set by the debacle of World War I. In the viola-
tions of man the notion of a personality which was equally
sacred with the aloof cosmos became anathema to him. But
even this disavowal rendered his emphasis on sacred space
so emphatic as to constitute a separate witness. Had the

divinity of personality ever manifested itself to him we would never have been given the divine cosmos he actually showed us through his humanly erroneous vision.

—◆◆◆—

As for myself, I found my sacred space and my true vocation in the same recognition, and for years this focus centered my energy and enabled me to survive the chaos of the world, when that world, once again at war, obtruded on my life. But the slipping away of region in the loss of love exposed me to search for a deeper synthesis, and I had to fight through to the sacrality of personality. That, for me, subsumed the instance of sacred space in the more sharply focused mandala, the person of Christ. Out of this flowed the Church, the collectivity of man in God. But it all began with sacred space.

—◆◆◆—

There is no time left to dwell upon the sacrality of personality as existentially co-equal with the sacrality of space, but it has been implicit in all these meditations, and it springs from the same principle of hierophany as sustains the cosmos. Jeffers would scoff, but for me everything finally came together only when that point was recognized.

—◆◆◆—

All things in due time. As writers the more urgent thing is for you to find your vocation. Somewhere there is a place that manifests for you the vibration of reality, your own deeply recognized sacred space, your true hierophany. It is the essence of regionalism, but don't dilute it with a name. When you find it, live in it, inhabit it, father its energies into you, found your world.

Meditation Eighteen: Birth of a Poet

During the first meditations, I spoke about the point of inception and its possibilities. Now we have reached the point of closure. *Closure.* It's a beautiful word. Because it comes when all is completed, the term doesn't seem to open possibilities at all, yet it has a kind of perfection that the inception point can't possess.

—◆◆◆—

Closure. The art of closing. One of the most important things in all forms of art is the closure. Many great works of art are fragmentary because the artist didn't have the particular insight into the closing. This goes for life too: to be able to finish in a perfect release and liberation which is the sign of completion. It is as if the life which is lived well in all its dimensions from beginning to end will have a close which follows beautifully and naturally.

—◆◆◆—

These meditations have been called "Birth of a Poet." Now the birth is over and the process has reached another dimension. We called these meditations a reflection on charismatic vocation, and spoke of that vocation as a calling. We dwelt many times on the whole meaning of the calling, what it is to be called, *vocare.* We spoke of surrender, call and surrender. We saw the vocation as the central

189

point of the life energies, and we spoke of the necessity to realize the essence of the vocation in order to seize the archetype which controls the whole. Your skills, remember, are limited, but the vocation itself knows no limit. It relates you to the collective life, and the vast energies of the world go into the fulfillment of that vocation. This is the reason that once you are established in your vocation you can transcend your natural skill.

— ♦♦♦ —

Unless you are deeply integrated in your vocation, you will not be able to sustain it. Only the vocation itself will be able to carry you through the afflictions which will come. Your skills can't do it, as they have nothing to do with your motivation, which comes from a different source.

— ♦♦♦ —

We spoke of the archetype of the hero, the necessity for maintaining an heroic consciousness. The collective cannot advance on its own. It has no possibility for evolution through itself. Only through the creative person can the collective evolve. This is why it reaches into the life of the individual and takes hold of the charismatic man. The collective cries out for the voice of deliverance which is buried in its guts. It evokes the creative personality which will carry it into its new destiny. And that is you.

— ♦♦♦ —

You will assume this calling at your peril, but you will avoid it at your peril too. Either way, it is difficult. You are destined for a role that is greater than yourself, and life will not let you back away from it. This is where your intrinsic beauty will emerge, because you will fulfill yourself in it. When you have done that, you can truly look back from the closing point and feel fulfilled.

— ♦♦♦ —

All along, we compared the artist's vocation to the religious life, seeing it as a way of serving not only yourself and the collective, but as a way of serving God. God—the source of all being, the great Orchestrator of the whole. We saw vocation as the key to meditation and contemplation, that which keeps you pure.

—◆◆◆—

I do not divide your life into a religious life and a secular life. I see your vocation as the heart of your religious life, and that the fulfilling of your vocation is the fulfilling of your religious life.

—◆◆◆—

We spoke of the ordeal of the American nation in its travail of emergence, and wondered at its creative destiny for the world. The nation is part of you, and you are part of the nation. Honor or despise it, the relationship remains. We spoke of the intrinsic qualities of the American nature. We spoke of the necessity for being aware of it and probing into that national archetype in order to come to terms with your vocation.

—◆◆◆—

In the last few meditations we went into the regional aspect, the spirit of place. We spoke of how the energies which are centered in place are also the energies which are crying out to you for fulfillment.

—◆◆◆—

My heart is afire with the joy of fulfillment. I am shaking from it. The consummation of a beautiful episode in my life. Yet there is always that note of sadness when something good ends. It is the essence of life in nature that when its forms pass away they leave a trace of their beauty so that we put our eyes forward to that place where beauty is eternal. Yet every minute is really that end. All the God there is, is right now. *All the God there is!* Nothing greater in heaven than right here, and we hold it in our hands. Right now we possess the sum of all reality and truth. To be able to see it, smell it, touch it . . .

—◆◆◆—

We have many views of heaven, but the mystics tell us that the meaning of beatitude is that all the potentiality of your whole being is realized in total *act*, forever. It is as if every impulsion you are capable of is ablaze instantaneously and permanently. Total awareness, total consciousness, total fulfillment. I believe it because I can taste it already. I know what it is like. When you let the core of your mind drop down over that inner being and sense that potentiality there, the vision is real. You can step back from your vocation for a moment, knowing that it is just a servitude in this life; but somewhere else there will be only the awareness, the total joy, the beautiful, spontaneous rapture of the indivisible gaze sharing its utter wholeness with you.

—◆◆◆—

O the close, the close, the beautiful close! The art of closure. Closing means a separation from, and yet a subsumption in and of. It has that beautiful paradoxical element in it, both fulfillment and separation. The art of closure is the art of acceptance, of saying yes to finality. It is difficult, for we cling so hard to those unrealized joys. We cover so much of what we need by the great pains which are put upon us by life, that we can't reach through and say *yes*. The only way to overcome a neurosis is to accept the pain which causes it. To accept it. *The acceptance.* In the acceptance comes the closure and the deliverance, the joy of release and liberation. Freedom in acceptance—that's a powerful thought, that freedom lies in acceptance. Yet there seems to be so much in our minds we need to know that we refuse to accept. We are stubborn, constantly attempting to reduce everything to our own mode of knowing. We refuse to accept unless we understand, and that is our error. If we chose to accept, understanding would be given to us.

—♦♦♦—

Go now into the great latitude that awaits you out there, the reality that is not closing but opening. Seize it in your two hands even as you embrace it and wrestle the meaning from it in your thirst. But never forget that only the acceptance at the close will yield the mystery of wholeness to you, the thing you desire most of all. You have to lose your life in order to save it. You have to expend yourself in order to find yourself. You gain your life only by giving it up.

Notes

¹ October 20, 1973. President Richard Nixon dismissed Special Prosecutor Archibald Cox for refusing to halt any further use of the courts in the Watergate investigation.

² On December 7, 1969, Brother Antoninus concluded a poetry reading at the University of California at Davis by taking off his monk's habit and returning to lay life as William Everson.

³ Joseph Campbell, *The Hero With a Thousand Faces* (Princeton: Princeton University Press, 1949). The term "monomyth" is a neologism in *Finnegans Wake*.

⁴ See Arthur Janov, *The Primal Scream* (New York: Putnam, 1970), and *The Primal Revolution* (New York: Simon and Schuster, 1972).

⁵ Italian educator Maria Montessori (1870-1952) developed a system of instructing young children wherein the fundamental aim was self-education by the children themselves, accompanied by special emphasis on the training of the senses.

⁶ Collected in *The Snow-Image and Uncollected Tales* (Columbus: Ohio State University Press, 1974).

⁷ The German Nikolaus von Cusa (1401-1464) was a cardinal, mathematician, and philosopher who attempted to replace Aristotelian logic with a sort of mysticism. See especially "De docta ignorantia" (1439-40), on the finite and the infinite.

⁸ Jeffers wrote "The Bloody Sire" in the summer of 1940.

⁹ William Everson, *The Hazards of Holiness* (Garden City: Doubleday, 1962).

¹⁰ See Everson, "The Uses of Imprecision" in *Robinson Jeffers: Fragments of an Older Fury* (Berkeley: Oyez, 1968), "A Conversation with Brother Antoninus" in *Earth Poetry: Selected Essays and Interviews, 1950-1977* (Berkeley: Oyez, 1980), and *Dionysus & the Beat: Four Letters on the Archetype* (Santa Barbara: Black Sparrow Press, 1977).

[11] See, for example, R. W. B. Lewis, *The American Adam* (Chicago: University of Chicago Press, 1955), and Leo Marx, *The Machine in the Garden* (New York: Oxford University Press, 1964).

[12] Henry David Thoreau, "Walking," *Excursions and Poems* (Boston: Houghton Mifflin and Company, 1893), p. 232.

[13] Carl Van Doren's short essay on Melville in the *Cambridge History of American Literature* in 1917 (followed in 1921 by the first full-length biography, *Herman Melville, Mariner and Mystic*, by Raymond Weaver) began the "Melville revival" of the 1920s and 1930s.

[14] W. H. Auden, ed., *The Criterion Book of Modern American Verse* (New York: Criterion Books, 1956), pp. 17-18.

[15] W. H. Auden's review of *The Oxford Book of Twentieth Century English Verse* (edited by Philip Larkin) appeared in the *San Francisco Chronicle*, "This World," April 29, 1973, p. 33.

[16] Robinson Jeffers, *Cawdor/Medea* (New York: New Directions, 1970), p. 29.

[17] Everson, *The Residual Years* (New York: New Directions, 1968), p. 90.

[18] Everson was interned as a conscientious objector in Camp Angel, Waldport, and Cascade Locks, both in Oregon, from January, 1943, to July, 1946.

[19] See Everson's preface to Robert Brophy, *Robinson Jeffers: Myth, Ritual, and Symbol in His Narrative Poems* (Cleveland: Case Western Reserve University Press, 1973), p. ix.

[20] Mircea Eliade, *Shamanism: Archaic Techniques of Ecstasy* (Princeton: Princeton University Press, 1964), and Andreas Lommel, *Shamanism: The Beginnings of Art* (New York: McGraw-Hill, 1966).

[21] Eric Neumann, *Art and the Creative Unconscious* (Princeton: Princeton University Press, 1959), pp. 177-78.

[22] Carlos Castaneda's books include *The Teachings of Don Juan, A Separate Reality, Journey to Ixtlan,* and *Tales of Power.*

[23] Charles A. Reich, *The Greening of America* (New York: Random House, 1970).

[24] See *The I Ching or Book of Changes* (Princeton: Princeton University Press, 1950).

[25] Gary Snyder received the Pulitzer Prize for Poetry in 1975 for his volume *Turtle Island* (New York: New Directions, 1974).

[26] See Everson's *Robinson Jeffers*. In addition, he has edited Jeffers' *Cawdor/Medea* (1970), *Californians* (1971), *The Alpine Christ* (1973), *Brides of the South Wind* (1974), and *The Double Axe* (with Bill Hotchkiss, 1978).

[27] Richard Aldington, ed., *The Spirit of Place: An Anthology Compiled From the Prose of D. H. Lawrence* (London: William Heinemann Ltd, 1935).

[28] Selma, California.

[29] Everson was in the Civilian Conservation Corps during 1933 and 1934.

[30] Jack Kerouac, *Big Sur* (New York: Farrar, Straus & Cudahy, Inc., 1962).

[31] Paul Shepard, *Man in the Landscape* (New York: Alfred Knopf, 1967), p. 33.

[32] *Ibid.*

[33] Everson, *The Residual Years* (New York: New Directions, 1968), p. 43.

[34] Robinson Jeffers, *The Selected Poetry* (New York: Random House, 1951). In his foreword, Jeffers writes that his "nature is cold and undiscriminating; she excited and focused it, gave it eyes and nerves and sympathies . . . A second piece of pure accident brought us to the Monterey coast mountains, where for the first time in my life I could see people living—amid magnificent unspoiled scenery—essentially as they did in the Idyls of the Sagas, or in Homer's Ithaca."

[35] Mircea Eliade, *The Sacred and the Profane* (New York: Harper & Row, 1961), pp. 20-21.

[36] Included in "Descent to the Dead" section of Jeffers' *Give Your Heart to the Hawks* (1933); see Jeffers' *Selected Poetry*.

Printed March 1982 in Santa Barbara and Ann Arbor
for the Black Sparrow Press by Graham Mackintosh
& Edwards Brothers, Inc. Design by Barbara Martin.
This edition is published in paper wrappers; there
are 750 hardcover trade copies; 250 hardcover
copies have been numbered & signed by the author;
& there are 50 copies handbound in boards by
Earle Gray, each containing a holograph poem by
William Everson.

Photo: Robert Turney

WILLIAM EVERSON was born in 1912 at Sacramento, California, and grew up in the San Joaquin Valley. He attended Fresno State College where he encountered the verse of Robinson Jeffers, crystalizing his own vocation as a poet. In World War II he served as a conscientious objector, then returned to the Bay Area to join the group of poets around Kenneth Rexroth, nucleus of the famed San Francisco Renaissance. In 1949 he converted to Catholicism and in 1951 entered the Dominican Order, taking the name Brother Antoninus. In 1969, after eighteen years as a lay brother, he left the Dominicans to marry. He lives in the mountains with his wife and son near the University of California at Santa Cruz, where he is poet in residence.

Everson has published over forty-five books of verse and scholarship. His honors include a Guggenheim Fellowship in 1949, a Pulitzer Prize nomination in 1959, the Commonwealth Club of California's Silver Medal in 1967, the Shelley Memorial Award plus the Book of the Year Award of the Conference on Christianity and Literature (an affiliate of the Modern Language Association) in 1978, and a National Endowment for the Arts Fellowship in 1982. He is also a hand-press printer of distinction.

LEE BARTLETT's poems, reviews, and scholarly articles have appeared in leading journals, and his assessment of the year's critical work on contemporary poetry appears annually in *American Literary Scholarship*. Bartlett's most recent books include *Letters to Christopher: Stephen Spender's Letters to Christopher Isherwood, 1929-1939* (Black Sparrow Press, 1980) and *The Beats: Essays in Criticism* (McFarland, 1981). Currently he is living in Albuquerque with his wife, the poet Mary Dougherty, where he teaches American Literature and is on the Creative Writing Faculty at the University of New Mexico.

DATE DUE